CAMBRIDGE LIBRARY COLLECTION

Books of enduring scholarly value

English Men of Letters

In the 1870s, Macmillan publishers began to issue a series of books called
'English Men of Letters' – biographies of English writers by other English
writers. The general editor of the series was the journalist, critic, politician,
and supporter (and later biographer) of Gladstone, John Morley (1838–
1923). The aim was to provide a short introduction to each subject and his
works, but also that the life should illuminate the works, and vice versa. The
subjects range chronologically from Chaucer to Thackeray and Dickens, and
an important feature of the series is that many of the authors (Henry James
on Hawthorne, Ward on Dickens) were discussing writers of the previous
generation, and some (Trollope on Thackeray) had even known their subjects
personally. The series exemplifies the British approach to literary biography
and criticism at the end of the nineteenth century, and also reveals which
authors were at that time regarded as canonical.

Daniel Defoe

Published in the first series of English Men of Letters in 1879, a time
when a complete edition of Daniel Defoe's works was yet to be collated,
this biograhical account by William Minto (1845–93) was a significant
achievement in literary scholarship as well as an engaging portrait of a
colourful and outspoken polemicist. Himself a journalist and essayist for the
pioneering *Pall Mall Gazette* and the *Daily News*, Minto combines the critical
insight of a literary scholar with the empathy and understanding of a fellow
writer. Spanning the novelist's entire life (c. 1659–1731), from the passions
of his youth to the publication of *Robinson Crusoe*, his 'later journalistic
labours' and the impact of literary success, this biography tells how Defoe
disproved the rule that the lives of men of letters are rarely eventful.

T0381727

Cambridge University Press has long been a pioneer in the reissuing of out-of-print titles from its own backlist, producing digital reprints of books that are still sought after by scholars and students but could not be reprinted economically using traditional technology. The Cambridge Library Collection extends this activity to a wider range of books which are still of importance to researchers and professionals, either for the source material they contain, or as landmarks in the history of their academic discipline.

Drawing from the world-renowned collections in the Cambridge University Library, and guided by the advice of experts in each subject area, Cambridge University Press is using state-of-the-art scanning machines in its own Printing House to capture the content of each book selected for inclusion. The files are processed to give a consistently clear, crisp image, and the books finished to the high quality standard for which the Press is recognised around the world. The latest print-on-demand technology ensures that the books will remain available indefinitely, and that orders for single or multiple copies can quickly be supplied.

The Cambridge Library Collection will bring back to life books of enduring scholarly value (including out-of-copyright works originally issued by other publishers) across a wide range of disciplines in the humanities and social sciences and in science and technology.

Daniel Defoe

WILLIAM MINTO

CAMBRIDGE
UNIVERSITY PRESS

CAMBRIDGE UNIVERSITY PRESS

Cambridge, New York, Melbourne, Madrid, Cape Town,
Singapore, São Paolo, Delhi, Tokyo, Mexico City

Published in the United States of America by Cambridge University Press, New York

www.cambridge.org
Information on this title: www.cambridge.org/9781108034715

© in this compilation Cambridge University Press 2011

This edition first published 1879
This digitally printed version 2011

ISBN 978-1-108-03471-5 Paperback

English Men of Letters

EDITED BY JOHN MORLEY

DANIEL DEFOE

DANIEL DEFOE

BY

WILLIAM MINTO

London

MACMILLAN AND CO

1879

LONDON :
R . CLAY, SONS, AND TAYLOR,
BREAD STREET HILL.

PREFACE.

THERE are three considerable biographies of Defoe—the first, by George Chalmers, published in 1786; the second by Walter Wilson, published in 1830; the third, by William Lee, published in 1869. All three are thorough and painstaking works, justified by independent research and discovery. The labour of research in the case of an author supposed to have written some two hundred and fifty separate books and pamphlets, very few of them under his own name, is naturally enormous; and when it is done, the results are open to endless dispute. Probably two men could not be found who would read through the vast mass of contemporary anonymous and pseudonymous print, and agree upon a complete list of Defoe's writings. Fortunately, however, for those who wish to get a clear idea of his life and character, the identification is not pure guess-work on internal evidence. He put his own name or initials to some of his productions, and treated the authorship of

others as open secrets. Enough is ascertained as his,
to provide us with the means for a complete understanding of his opinions and his conduct. It is Defoe's
misfortune that his biographers on the large scale have
occupied themselves too much with subordinate details,
and have been misled from a true appreciation of
his main lines of thought and action by religious,
political, and hero-worshipping bias. For the following
sketch, taking Mr. Lee's elaborate work as my chronological guide, I have read such of Defoe's undoubted
writings as are accessible in the Library of the British
Museum—there is no complete collection, I believe,
in existence—and endeavoured to connect them and
him with the history of the time.

W. M.

January 1879.

CONTENTS.

CHAPTER VI.

CHAPTER VII.

CHAPTER VIII.

CHAPTER IX.

CHAPTER X.

DANIEL DEFOE

CHAPTER I.

THE life of a man of letters is not as a rule eventful. It may be rich in spiritual experiences, but it seldom is rich in active adventure. We ask his biographer to tell us what were his habits of composition, how he talked, how he bore himself in the discharge of his duties to his family, his neighbours, and himself; what were his beliefs on the great questions that concern humanity. We desire to know what he said and wrote, not what he did beyond the study and the domestic or the social circle. The chief external facts in his career are the dates of the publication of his successive books.

Daniel Defoe is an exception to this rule. He was a man of action as well as a man of letters. The writing of the books which have given him immortality was little more than an accident in his career, a comparatively trifling and casual item in the total expenditure of his many-sided energy. He was nearly sixty when he wrote *Robinson Crusoe*. Before that event he had been a rebel, a merchant, a manufacturer, a writer of popular satires in verse, a bankrupt; had acted as secretary to a public commission, been employed in secret services by five successive Administrations, written innumerable pamphlets, and edited more than one newspaper. He had led in fact as adventurous a life as any of his own heroes, and had met quickly succeeding difficulties with equally ready and fertile ingenuity.

For many of the incidents in Defoe's life we are indebted to himself. He had all the vaingloriousness of exuberant vitality, and was animated in the recital of his own adventures. Scattered throughout his various works are the materials for a tolerably complete autobiography. This is in one respect an advantage for any one who attempts to give an account of his life. But it has a counterbalancing disadvantage in the circumstance that there is grave reason to doubt his veracity. Defoe was a great story-teller in more senses than one. We can hardly believe a word that he says about himself without independent confirmation.

Defoe was born in London, in 1661. It is a characteristic circumstance that his name is not his own, except in the sense that it was assumed by himself. The name of his father, who was a butcher in the parish of St. Giles, Cripplegate, was Foe. His grandfather was a Northamptonshire yeoman. In his *True Born Englishman*, Defoe spoke very contemptuously of families that professed to have come over with " the Norman bastard," defying them to prove whether their ancestors were drummers or colonels; but apparently he was not above the vanity of making the world believe that he himself was of Norman-French origin. Yet such was the restless energy of the man that he could not leave even his adopted name alone; he seems to have been about forty when he first changed his signature "D. Foe" into the surname of "Defoe;" but his patient biographer, Mr. Lee, has found several later instances of his subscribing himself "D. Foe," "D. F.," and "De Foe" in alternation with the "Daniel De Foe," or "Daniel Defoe," which has become his accepted name in literature.

In middle age, when Defoe was taunted with his want of learning, he retorted that if he was a blockhead it was not the fault of his father, who had "spared nothing in his education that might qualify him to match the accurate Dr. Browne, or the learned Observator." His father was a Nonconformist, a member of the congregation of Dr. Annesley, and the son was originally intended for the Dissenting ministry. "It was his disaster," he said afterwards, "first to be set apart for, and then to be set apart from, that sacred employ." He was placed at an academy for the training of ministers at the age, it is supposed, of about fourteen, and probably remained there for the full course of five years. He has himself explained why, when his training was completed, he did not proceed to the office of the pulpit, but changed his views and resolved to engage in business as a hose-merchant. The sum of the explanation is that the ministry seemed to him at that time to be neither honourable, agreeable, nor profitable. It was degraded, he thought, by the entrance of men who had neither physical nor intellectual qualification for it, who had received out of a denominational fund only such an education as made them pedants rather than Christian gentlemen of high learning, and who had consequently to submit to shameful and degrading practices in their efforts to obtain congregations and subsistence. Besides, the behaviour of congregations to their ministers, who were dependent, was often objectionable and un-Christian. And finally, far-flown birds having fine feathers, the prizes of the ministry in London were generally given to strangers, "eminent ministers *called* from all parts of England," some even from Scotland, finding acceptance in the metropolis before having received any formal ordination.

Though the education of his " fund-bred " companions, as he calls them, at Mr. Morton's Academy in Newington Green, was such as to excite Defoe's contempt, he bears testimony to Mr. Morton's excellence as a teacher, and instances the names of several pupils who did credit to his labours. In one respect Mr. Morton's system was better than that which then prevailed at the Universities ; all dissertations were written and all disputations held in English ; and hence it resulted, Defoe says, that his pupils, though they were "not destitute in the languages," were " made masters of the English tongue, and more of them excelled in that particular than of any school at that time." Whether Defoe obtained at Newington the rudiments of all the learning which he afterwards claimed to be possessed of, we do not know ; but the taunt frequently levelled at him by University men of being an "illiterate fellow" and no scholar, was one that he bitterly resented, and that drew from him many protestations and retorts. In 1705, he angrily challenged John Tutchin "to translate with him any Latin, French, or Italian author, and after that to retranslate them crosswise for twenty pounds each book ; " and he replied to Swift, who had spoken of him scornfully as "an illiterate fellow, whose name I forget," that "he had been in his time pretty well master of five languages, and had not lost them yet, though he wrote no bill at his door, nor set Latin quotations on the front of the *Review.*" To the end of his days Defoe could not forget this taunt of want of learning. In one of the papers in *Applebee's Journal* identified by Mr. Lee (below, Chapter VIII.), he discussed what is to be understood by "learning," and drew the following sketch of his own attainments :—

"I remember an Author in the World some years ago, who was generally upbraided with Ignorance, and called an 'Illiterate Fellow,' by some of the *Beau-Monde* of the last Age. . . .

"I happened to come into this Person's Study once, and I found him busy translating a Description of the Course of the River Boristhenes, out of *Bleau's* Geography, written in *Spanish.* Another Time I found him translating some Latin Paragraphs out of *Leubinitz Theatri Cometici*, being a learned Discourse upon Comets ; and that I might see whether it was genuine, I looked on some part of it that he had finished, and found by it that he understood the Latin very well, and had perfectly taken the sense of that difficult Author. In short, I found he understood the *Latin*, the *Spanish*, the *Italian*, and could read the *Greek*, and I knew before that he spoke *French* fluently—*yet this Man was no Scholar.*

"As to Science, on another Occasion, I heard him dispute (in such a manner as surprised me) upon the motions of the Heavenly Bodies, the Distance, Magnitude, Revolutions, and especially the Influences of the Planets, the Nature and probable Revolutions of Comets, the excellency of the New Philosophy, and the like ; *but this Man was no Scholar.*

"In Geography and History he had all the World at his Finger's ends. He talked of the most distant Countries with an inimitable Exactness ; and changing from one Place to another, the Company thought, of every Place or Country he named, that certainly he must have been born there. He knew not only where every Thing was, but what everybody did in every Part of the World ; I mean, what Businesses, what Trade, what Manufacture, was carrying on in every Part of the World ; and had the History of almost all the Nations of the World in his Head,—*yet this Man was no Scholar.*

"This put me upon wondering, ever so long ago, what this *strange Thing* called a Man of Learning *was,* and what is it that constitutes a *Scholar ?* For, *said I,* here's a man speaks five Languages and reads the Sixth, is a master of Astronomy, Geography, History, and abundance of other useful Knowledge, (which I do not mention, that you may not guess at the Man, who is too Modest to desire it,) and yet, they say *this Man is no Scholar.*"

How much of this learning Defoe acquired at school, and how much he picked up afterwards under the pressure of the necessities of his business, it is impossible to determine, but at any rate it was at least as good a qualification for writing on public affairs as the more limited and accurate scholarship of his academic rivals. Whatever may have been the extent of his knowledge when he passed from Mr. Morton's tuition, qualified but no longer willing to become a Dissenting preacher, he did not allow it to rust unused ; he at once mobilised his forces for active service. They were keen politicians, naturally, at the Newington Academy, and the times furnished ample materials for their discussions. As Nonconformists they were very closely affected by the struggle between Charles II. and the defenders of Protestantism and popular liberties. What part Defoe took in the excitement of the closing years of the reign of Charles must be matter of conjecture, but there can be little doubt that he was active on the popular side. He had but one difference then, he afterwards said in one of his tracts, with his party. He

would not join them in wishing for the success of
the Turks in besieging Vienna, because, though the
Austrians were Papists and though the Turks were
ostensibly on the side of the Hungarian reformers
whom the Austrian Government had persecuted, he
had read the history of the Turks and could not pray
for their victory over Christians of any denomination.
" Though then but a young man, and a younger author "
(this was in 1683), "he opposed it and wrote against it,
which was taken very unkindly indeed." From these
words it would seem that Defoe had thus early begun
to write pamphlets on questions of the hour. As he
was on the weaker side, and any writing might have
cost him his life, it is probable that he did not put his
name to any of these tracts ; none of them have been
identified ; but his youth was strangely unlike his
mature manhood if he was not justified in speaking of
himself as having been then an "author." Nor was
he content merely with writing. It would have been
little short of a miracle if his restless energy had
allowed him to lie quiet while the air was thick with
political intrigue. We may be sure that he had a voice
in some of the secret associations in which plans were
discussed of armed resistance to the tyranny of the
King. We have his own word for it that he took part
in the Duke of Monmouth's rising, when the whips of
Charles were exchanged for the scorpions of James.
He boasted of this when it became safe to do so, and
the truth of the boast derives incidental confirmation
from the fact that the names of three of his fellow-
students at Newington appear in the list of the victims
of Jeffreys and Kirke.

Escaping the keen hunt that was made for all

participators in the rebellion, Defoe towards the close
of 1685 began business as a hosier or hose-factor in
Freeman's Court, Cornhill. The precise nature of his
trade has been disputed; and it does not particularly
concern us here. When taunted afterwards with having
been apprentice to a hosier, he indignantly denied the
fact, and explained that though he had been a trader in
hosiery he had never been a shopkeeper. A passing
illustration in his *Essay on Projects*, drawn from his own
experience, shows that he imported goods in the course
of his business from abroad; he speaks of sometimes
having paid more in insurance premios than he had
cleared by a voyage. From a story which he tells in
his *Complete English Tradesman*, recalling the cleverness
with which he defeated an attempt to outwit him about
a consignment of brandy, we learn that his business
sometimes took him to Spain. This is nearly all that
we know about his first adventure in trade, except that
after seven years, in 1692, he had to flee from his
creditors. He hints in one of his *Reviews* that this misfortune was brought about by the frauds of swindlers,
and it deserves to be recorded that he made the honourable boast that he afterwards paid off his obligations.
The truth of the boast is independently confirmed
by the admission of a controversial enemy, that very
Tutchin whom he challenged to translate Latin with
him. That Defoe should have referred so little to his
own experience in the *Complete English Tradesman*, a
series of Familiar Letters which he published late in life
"for the instruction of our Inland Tradesmen, and
especially of Young Beginners," is accounted for when
we observe the class of persons to whom the letters
were addressed. He distinguishes with his usual clear-

ness between the different ranks of those employed in the production and exchange of goods, and intimates that his advice is not intended for the highest grade of traders, the merchants, whom he defines by what he calls the vulgar expression, as being "such as trade beyond sea." Although he was eloquent in many books and pamphlets in upholding the dignity of trade, and lost no opportunity of scoffing at pretentious gentility he never allows us to forget that this was the grade to which he himself belonged, and addresses the petty trader from a certain altitude. He speaks in the preface to the *Complete Tradesman* of unfortunate creatures who have blown themselves up in trade, whether "for want of wit or from too much wit;" but lest he should be supposed to allude to his own misfortunes, he does not say that he miscarried himself but that he "had seen in a few years experience many young tradesmen miscarry." At the same time it is fair to conjecture that when Defoe warns the young tradesman against fancying himself a politician or a man of letters, running off to the coffee-house when he ought to be behind the counter, and reading Virgil and Horace when he should be busy over his journal and his ledger, he was glancing at some of the causes which conduced to his own failure as a merchant. And when he cautions the beginner against going too fast, and holds up to him as a type and exemplar the carrier's waggon, which "keeps wagging and always goes on," and "as softly as it goes" can yet in time go far, we may be sure that he was thinking of the over-rashness with which he had himself embarked in speculation.

There can be no doubt that eager and active as Defoe was in his trading enterprises, he was not so wrapt up

in them as to be an unconcerned spectator of the intense
political life of the time.   When King James aimed a
blow at the Church of England by removing the religious
disabilities of all dissenters, Protestant and Catholic,
in his Declaration of Indulgence, some of Defoe's co-
religionists were ready to catch at the boon without
thinking of its consequences.   He differed from them,
he afterwards stated, and "as he used to say that
he had rather the Popish House of Austria should
ruin the Protestants in Hungaria, than the infidel
House of Ottoman should ruin both Protestants and
Papists by overrunning Germany," so now "he told
the Dissenters he had rather the Church of England
should pull our clothes off by fines and forfeitures, than
the Papists should fall both upon the Church and the
Dissenters, and pull our skins off by fire and faggot."
He probably embodied these conclusions of his vigorous
common sense in a pamphlet, though no pamphlet on
the subject known for certain to be his has been preserved.   Mr. Lee is over-rash in identifying as Defoe's
a quarto sheet of that date entitled " A Letter containing some Reflections on His Majesty's declaration for
Liberty of Conscience."   Defoe may have written many
pamphlets on the stirring events of the time, which have
not come down to us.   It may have been then that he
acquired, or made a valuable possession by practice, that
marvellous facility with his pen which stood him in
such stead in after life.   It would be no wonder if he
wrote dozens of pamphlets, every one of which disappeared.   The pamphlet then occupied the place of the
newspaper leading article.   The newspapers of the time
were veritable chronicles of news, and not organs of
opinion.   The expression of opinion was not then asso-

ciated with the dissemination of facts and rumours. A man who wished to influence public opinion wrote a pamphlet, small or large, a single leaf or a tract of a few pages, and had it hawked about the streets and sold in the bookshops. These pamphlets issued from the press in swarms, were thrown aside when read, and hardly preserved except by accident. That Defoe, if he wrote any or many, should not have reprinted them when fifteen years afterwards he published a collection of his works, is intelligible; he republished only such of his tracts as had not lost their practical interest. If, however, we indulge in the fancy, warranted so far by his describing himself as having been a young "author" in 1683, that Defoe took an active part in polemical literature under Charles and James, we must remember that the censorship of the press was then active, and that Defoe must have published under greater disadvantages than those who wrote on the side of the Court.

At the Revolution, in 1688, Defoe lost no time in making his adhesion to the new monarch conspicuous. He was, according to Oldmixon, one of "a royal regiment of volunteer horse, made up of the chief citizens, who, being gallantly mounted and richly accoutred, were led by the Earl of Monmouth, now Earl of Peterborough, and attended their Majesties from Whitehall," to a banquet given by the Lord Mayor and Corporation of the City Three years afterwards, on the occasion of the Jacobite plot in which Lord Preston was the leading figure, he published the first pamphlet that is known for certain to be his. It is in verse, and is entitled *A New Discovery of an Old Intrigue, a Satire levelled at Treachery and Ambition.* In the preface, the author said that "he had never drawn his pen before," and that he would never write again unless this effort produced a visible reformation. If we take this literally, we must suppose that his claim to have been an author eighteen years before had its origin in his fitful vanity. The literary merits of the satire, when we compare it with the powerful verse of Dryden's *Absalom and Achitophel*, to which he refers in the exordium, are not great. Defoe prided himself upon his verse, and in a catalogue of the Poets in one of his later pieces assigned himself the special province of "lampoon." He possibly believed that his clever doggerel was a better title to immortality than *Robinson Crusoe*. The immediate popular effect of his satires gave some encouragement to this belief, but they are comparatively dull reading for posterity. The clever hits at living City functionaries, indicated by their initials and nicknames, the rough ridicule and the biting innuendo, were telling in their day, but the lampoons have perished with their objects. The local celebrity of Sir Ralph and Sir Peter, Silly Will and Captain Tom the Tailor, has vanished, and Defoe's hurried and formless lines, incisive as their vivid force must have been, are not redeemed from dulness for modern readers by the few bright epigrams with which they are besprinkled.

CHAPTER II.

DEFOE's first business catastrophe happened about 1692. He is said to have temporarily absconded, and to have parleyed with his creditors from a distance till they agreed to accept a composition. Bristol is named as having been his place of refuge, and there is a story that he was known there as the Sunday Gentleman, because he appeared on that day and that day only in fashionable attire, being kept indoors during the rest of the week by fear of the bailiffs. But he was of too buoyant a temperament to sink under his misfortune from the sense of having brought it on himself, and the cloud soon passed away. A man so fertile in expedients, and ready, according to his own ideal of a thorough-bred trader, to turn himself to anything, could not long remain unemployed. He had various business offers, and among others an invitation from some merchants to settle at Cadiz as a commission agent, "with offers of very good commissions." But Providence, he tells us, and, we may add, a shrewd confidence in his own powers, "placed a secret aversion in his mind to quitting England upon any account, and made him refuse the best offers of that kind." He stayed at home, "to be

concerned with some eminent persons in proposing ways
and means to the Government for raising money to
supply the occasions of the war then newly begun."
He also wrote a vigorous and loyal pamphlet, entitled,
*The Englishman's Choice and True Interest: in the
vigorous prosecution of the war against France, and
serving K. William and Q. Mary, and acknowledging
their right.* As a reward for his literary or his finan-
cial services or for both, he was appointed "without
the least application" of his own, Accountant to the
Commissioners of the Glass Duty, and held this post
till the duty was abolished in 1699.

From 1694 to the end of William's reign was the
most prosperous and honourable period in Defoe's life.
His services to the Government did not absorb the
whole of his restless energy. He still had time for
private enterprise, and started a manufactory of bricks
and pantiles at Tilbury, where, Mr. Lee says, judging
from fragments recently dug up, he made good sound
sonorous bricks, although according to another authority
such a thing was impossible out of any material existing
in the neighbourhood. Anyhow, Defoe prospered, and
set up a coach and a pleasure-boat. Nor must we forget
what is so much to his honour, that he set himself to pay
his creditors in full, voluntarily disregarding the composition which they had accepted. In 1705 he was able
to boast that he had reduced his debts in spite of many
difficulties from 17,000*l.* to 5,000*l.*, but these sums
included liabilities resulting from the failure of his
pantile factory.

Defoe's first conspicuous literary service to King
William, after he obtained Government employment,
was a pamphlet on the question of a Standing Army

raised after the Peace of Ryswick in 1697. This Pen
and Ink War, as he calls it, which followed close on
the heels of the great European struggle, had been
raging for some time before Defoe took the field. Hosts
of writers had appeared to endanger the permanence of
the triumph of William's arms and diplomacy by de-
manding the disbandment of his tried troops, as being
a menace to domestic liberties. Their arguments had
been encountered by no less zealous champions of the
King's cause. The battle, in fact, had been won when
Defoe issued his *Argument showing that a Standing
Army, with consent of Parliament, is not inconsistent
with a Free Government.* He was able to boast in his
preface that "if books and writings would not, God be
thanked the Parliament would confute" his adversaries.
Nevertheless, though coming late in the day, Defoe's
pamphlet was widely read, and must have helped to
consolidate the victory.

Thus late in life did Defoe lay the first stone of his
literary reputation. He was now in the thirty-eighth
year of his age, his controversial genius in full vigour,
and his mastery of language complete. None of his subsequent tracts surpass this as a piece of trenchant and
persuasive reasoning. It shows at their very highest his
marvellous powers of combining constructive with destructive criticism. He dashes into the lists with good-
humoured confidence, bearing the banner of clear common
sense, and disclaiming sympathy with extreme persons of
either side. He puts his case with direct and plausible
force, addressing his readers vivaciously as plain people
like himself, among whom as reasonable men there cannot
be two opinions. He cuts rival arguments to pieces
with dexterous strokes, representing them as the

confused reasoning of well-meaning but dull intellects, and dances with lively mockery on the fragments. If the authors of such arguments knew their own minds, they would be entirely on his side. He echoes the pet prejudices of his readers as the props and mainstays of his thesis, and boldly laughs away misgivings of which they are likely to be half ashamed. He makes no parade of logic; he is only a plain freeholder like the mass whom he addresses, though he knows twenty times as much as many writers of more pretension. He never appeals to passion or imagination; what he strives to enlist on his side is homely self-interest, and the ordinary sense of what is right and reasonable. There is little regularity of method in the development of his argument; that he leaves to more anxious and elaborate masters of style. For himself he is content to start from a bold and clear statement of his own opinion, and proceeds buoyantly and discursively to engage and scatter his enemies as they turn up, without the least fear of being able to fight his way back to his original base. He wrote for a class to whom a prolonged intellectual operation, however comprehensive and complete, was distasteful. To persuade the mass of the freeholders was his object, and for such an object there are no political tracts in the language at all comparable to Defoe's. He bears some resemblance to Cobbett, but he had none of Cobbett's brutality; his faculties were more adroit, and his range of vision infinitely wider. Cobbett was a demagogue, Defoe a popular statesman. The one was qualified to lead the people, the other to guide them. Cobbett is contained in Defoe as the less is contained in the greater.

King William obtained a standing army from Parliament, but not so large an army as he wished, and it was soon afterwards still further reduced. Meantime, Defoe employed his pen in promoting objects which were dear to the King's heart. His *Essay on Projects*—which "relate to Civil Polity as well as matters of negoce "— was calculated, in so far as it advocated joint-stock enterprise, to advance one of the objects of the statesmen of the Revolution, the committal of the moneyed classes to the established Government, and against a dynasty which might plausibly be mistrusted of respect for visible accumulations of private wealth. Defoe's projects were of an extremely varied kind. The classification was not strict. His spirited definition of the word "projects" included Noah's Ark and the Tower of Babel, as well as Captain Phipps's scheme for raising the wreck of a Spanish ship laden with silver. He is sometimes credited with remarkable shrewdness in having anticipated in this Essay some of the greatest public improvements of modern times—the protection of seamen, the higher education of women, the establishment of banks and benefit societies, the construction of highways. But it is not historically accurate to give him the whole credit of these conceptions. Most of them were floating about at the time, so much so that he had to defend himself against a charge of plagiarism, and few of them have been carried out in accordance with the essential features of his plans. One remarkable circumstance in Defoe's projects, which we may attribute either to his own natural bent or to his compliance with the King's humour, is the extent to which he advocated Government interference. He proposed, for example, an income-tax, and the appointment of a commission who should travel through the country and

ascertain by inquiry that the tax was not evaded. In
making this proposal he shows an acquaintance with
private incomes in the City, which raises some suspicion
as to the capacity in which he was "associated with
certain eminent persons in proposing ways and means
to the Government." In his article on Banks, he expresses himself dissatisfied that the Government did not
fix a maximum rate of interest for the loans made by
chartered banks; they were otherwise, he complained,
of no assistance to the poor trader, who might as well
go to the goldsmiths as before. His Highways project
was a scheme for making national highways on a scale
worthy of Baron Haussmann. There is more fervid
imagination and daring ingenuity than business talent
in Defoe's essay; if his trading speculations were conducted with equal rashness, it is not difficult to understand their failure. The most notable of them are the
schemes of a dictator, rather than of the adviser of a
free Government. The essay is chiefly interesting as a
monument of Defoe's marvellous force of mind, and
strange mixture of steady sense with incontinent flighti-
ness. There are ebullient sallies in it which we generally find only in the productions of madmen and
charlatans, and yet it abounds in suggestions which
statesmen might profitably have set themselves with
due adaptations to carry into effect. The *Essay on
Projects* might alone be adduced in proof of Defoe's
title to genius.

One of the first projects to which the Government of
the Revolution addressed itself was the reformation of
manners—a purpose at once commendable in itself and
politically useful as distinguishing the new Government
from the old. Even while the King was absent in

Ireland at the beginning of his reign, the Queen issued a letter calling upon all justices of the peace and other servants of the Crown to exert themselves in suppressing the luxuriant growth of vice, which had been fostered by the example of the Court of Charles. On the conclusion of the war in 1697, William issued a most elaborate proclamation to the same effect, and an address was voted by Parliament, asking his Majesty to see that wickedness was discouragad in high places. The lively pamphlet in which Defoe lent his assistance to the good work, entitled *The Poor Man's Plea*, was written in the spirit of the parliamentary address. It was of no use to pass laws and make declarations and proclamations for the reform of the common *plebeii*, the poor man pleaded, so long as the mentors of the laws were themselves corrupt. His argument was spiced with amusing anecdotes to show the prevalence of swearing and drunkenness among members of the judicial bench. Defoe appeared several times afterwards in the character of a reformer of manners, sometimes in verse, sometimes in prose. When the retort was made that his own manners were not perfect, he denied that this invalidated the worth of his appeal, but at the same time challenged his accusers to prove him guilty of any of the vices that he had satirised.

It is impossible now to ascertain what induced Defoe to break with the Dissenters, among whom he had been brought up, but break with them he did in his pamphlet against the practice of *Occasional Conformity*. This practice of occasionally taking communion with the Established Church, as a qualification for public office, had grown up after the Revolution, and had attracted very little notice till a Dissenting lord mayor, after attending church one Sunday forenoon, went in the afternoon with all the insignia of his office to a Conventicle. Defoe's objection to this is indicated in his quotation, " If the Lord be God, follow Him, but if Baal, then follow him." A man, he contended, who could reconcile it with his conscience to attend the worship of the Church, had no business to be a Dissenter. Occasional conformity was " either a sinful act in itself, or else his dissenting before was sinful." The Dissenters naturally did not like this intolerant logical dilemma, and resented its being forced upon them by one of their own number against a practical compromise to which the good sense of the majority of them assented. No reply was made to the pamphlet when first issued in 1698, and two or three years afterwards Defoe, exulting in the unanswerable logic of his position, reprinted it with a prefatory challenge to Mr. Howe, an eminent dissenting minister. During the next reign, however, when a bill was introduced to prohibit the practice of occasional conformity, Defoe strenuously wrote against it as a breach of the Toleration Act and a measure of persecution. In strict logic it is possible to make out a case for his consistency, but the reasoning must be fine, and he cannot be acquitted of having in the first instance practically justified a persecution which he afterwards condemned. In neither case does he point at the repeal of the Test Act as his object, and it is impossible to explain his attitude in both cases on the ground of principle. However much he objected to see the sacrament taken as a matter of form, it was hardly his province, in the circumstances in which Dissenters then stood, to lead an outcry against the practice; and if he considered it scandalous and

sinful, he could not with much consistency protest against
the prohibition of it as an act of persecution. Of this no
person was better aware than Defoe himself, and it is
a curious circumstance that, in his first pamphlet on the
bill for putting down occasional conformity, he ridiculed
the idea of its being persecution to suppress politic or
state Dissenters, and maintained that the bill did not
concern true Dissenters at all. To this, however, we
must refer again in connexion with his celebrated tract,
The Shortest Way with Dissenters.

The troubles into which the European system was
plunged by the death of the childless King of Spain,
and that most dramatic of historical surprises, the
bequest of his throne by a death-bed will to the Duke
of Anjou, the second grandson of Louis XIV., furnished
Defoe with a great opportunity for his controversial
genius. In Charles II.'s will, if the legacy was accepted,
William saw the ruin of a life-long policy. Louis,
though he was doubly pledged against acknowledging
the will, having renounced all pretensions to the throne
of Spain for himself and his heirs in the Treaty of the
Pyrenees, and consented in two successive treaties of
partition to a different plan of succession, did not long
hesitate ; the news that he had saluted his grandson as
King of Spain followed close upon the news of Charles's
death. The balance of the great Catholic Powers which
William had established by years of anxious diplomacy
and costly war, was toppled over by a stroke of the pen.
With Spain and Italy virtually added to his dominions,
the French King would now be supreme upon the Continent. Louis soon showed that this was his view of
what had happened, by saying that the Pyrenees had
ceased to exist. He gave a practical illustration of the

same view by seizing, with the authority of his grandson, the frontier towns of the Spanish Netherlands, which were garrisoned under a special treaty by Dutch troops. Though deeply enraged at the bad faith of the most Christian King, William was not dismayed. The stone which he had rolled up the hill with such effort had suddenly rolled down again, but he was eager to renew his labours. Before, however, he could act, he found himself, to his utter astonishment and mortification, paralysed by the attitude of the English Parliament. His alarm at the accession of a Bourbon to the Spanish throne was not shared by the ruling classes in England. They declared that they liked the Spanish King's will better than William's partition. France, they argued, would gain much less by a dynastic alliance with Spain, which would exist no longer than their common interests dictated, than by the complete acquisition of the Spanish provinces in Italy.

William lost no time in summoning a new Parliament. An overwhelming majority opposed the idea of vindicating the Partition Treaty by arms. They pressed him to send a message of recognition to Philip V. Even the occupation of the Flemish fortresses did not change their temper. That, they said, was the affair of the Dutch; it did not concern England. In vain William tried to convince them that the interests of the two Protestant States were identical. In the numerous pamphlets that were hatched by the ferment, it was broadly insinuated that the English people might pay too much for the privilege of having a Dutch King, who had done nothing for them that they could not have done for themselves, and who was perpetually sacrificing the interests of his adopted country to the necessities of his beloved Holland. What had England gained by the Peace of Ryswick? Was England to be dragged into another exhausting war, merely to secure a strong frontier for the Dutch? The appeal found ready listeners among a people in whose minds the recollections of the last war were still fresh, and who still felt the burdens it had left behind. William did not venture to take any steps to form an alliance against France, till a new incident emerged to shake the country from its mood of surly calculation. When James II. died and Louis recognised the Pretender as King of England, all thoughts of isolation from a Continental confederacy were thrown to the winds. William dissolved his Long Parliament, and found the new House as warlike as the former had been peaceful. " Of all the nations in the world," cried Defoe, in commenting on this sudden change of mood, " there is none that I know of so entirely governed by their humour as the English."

For ten months Defoe had been vehemently but vainly striving to accomplish by argument what had been wrought in an instant by the French King's insufferable insult. It is one of the most brilliant periods of his political activity. Comparatively undistinguished before, he now, at the age of forty, stepped into the foremost rank of publicists. He lost not a moment in throwing himself into the fray as the champion of the King's policy. Charles of Spain died on the 22nd of October, 1701 ; by the middle of November, a few days after the news had reached England, and before the French King's resolve to acknowledge the legacy was known, Defoe was ready with a pamphlet to the clear and stirring title of—*The Two Great questions considered.* I. *What the French King will do with respect to the Spanish Monarchy.* II. *What measures the English ought to take.* If the French King were wise, he argued, he would reject the dangerous gift for his grandson. But if he accepted it, England had no choice but to combine with her late allies the Emperor and the States, and compel the Duke of Anjou to withdraw his claims. This pamphlet being virulently attacked, and its author accused of bidding for a place at Court, Defoe made a spirited rejoinder, and seized the occasion to place his arguments in still clearer light. Between them the two pamphlets are a masterly exposition, from the point of view of English interests, of the danger of permitting the Will to be fulfilled. He tears the arguments of his opponents to pieces with supreme scorn. What matters it to us who is King of Spain? asks one adversary. As well ask, retorts Defoe, what it matters to us who is King of Ireland. All this talk about the Balance of Power, says another, is only "a shoeing-horn to draw on a standing army." We do not want an army; only let us make our fleet strong enough and we may defy the world; our militia is perfectly able to defend us against invasion. If our militia is so strong, is Defoe's reply, why should a standing-army make us fear for our domestic liberties? But if you object to a standing-army in England, avert the danger by subsidising allies and raising and paying troops in Germany and the Low Countries. Even if we are capable of beating off invasion, it is always wise policy to keep the war out of our own country, and not trust to such miracles as the dispersion of the Armada. In war, Defoe says, repeating a favourite axiom of his, "it is not the longest sword but the longest purse that conquers," and

if the French get the Spanish crown, they get the
richest trade in the world into their hands. The French
would prove better husbands of the wealth of Mexico
and Peru than the Spaniards. They would build fleets
with it, which would place our American plantations at
their mercy. Our own trade with Spain, one of the
most profitable fields for our enterprise, would at once
be ruined. Our Mediterranean trade would be burdened
with the impost of a toll at Gibraltar. In short Defoe
contended, if the French acquired the upper hand in
Spain, nothing but a miracle could save England from
becoming practically a French province.

Defoe's appeal to the sense of self-interest fell, however, upon deaf ears. No eloquence or ingenuity of
argument could have availed to stem the strong current
of growling prepossession. He was equally unsuccessful
in his attempt to touch deeper feelings by exhibiting
in a pamphlet, which is perhaps the ablest of the series,
*The danger of the Protestant Religion, from the present
prospect of a Religious War in Europe.* " Surely you
cannot object to a standing army for the defence of
your religion ? " he argued ; "for if you do, then you
stand convicted of valuing your liberties more than
your religion, which ought to be your first and highest
concern." Such scraps of rhetorical logic were but as
straws in the storm of anti-warlike passion that was
then raging. Nor did Defoe succeed in turning the
elections by addressing " to the good people of England" his *Six Distinguishing Characters of a Parliament Man,* or by protesting as a freeholder against
the levity of making the strife between the new and the
old East India Companies a testing question, when the
very existence of the kingdom was at stake. His

pamphlets were widely distributed, but he might as
soon have tried to check a tempest by throwing handfuls
of leaves into it. One great success, however, he had,
and that, strangely enough, in a direction in which it
was least to be anticipated. No better proof could be
given that the good-humoured magnanimity and sense
of fair-play on which English people pride themselves
is more than an empty boast than the reception
accorded to Defoe's *True-Born Englishman.* King
William's unpopularity was at its height. A party
writer of the time had sought to inflame the general
dislike to his Dutch favourites by " a vile pamphlet in
abhorred verse," entitled *The Foreigners,* in which they are
loaded with scurrilous insinuations. It required no ordinary courage in the state of the national temper at that
moment to venture upon the line of retort that Defoe
adopted. What were the English, he demanded, that they
should make a mock of foreigners ? They were the most
mongrel race that ever lived upon the face of the earth ;
there was no such thing as a true-born Englishman ;
they were all the offspring of foreigners ; what was
more, of the scum of foreigners.

> " For Englishmen to boast of generation
> Cancels their knowledge, and lampoons the nation.
> A true-born Englishman 's a contradiction,
> In speech an irony, in fact a fiction.
>
> *   *   *   *
> And here begins the ancient pedigree
> That so exalts our poor nobility.
> 'Tis that from some French trooper they derive,
> Who with the Norman bastard did arrive ;
> The trophies of the families appear,
> Some show the sword, the bow, and some the spear

Which their great ancestor, forsooth, did wear.
These in the herald's register remain,
Their noble mean extraction to explain,
Yet who the hero was no man can tell,
Whether a drummer or a colonel;
The silent record blushes to reveal
Their undescended dark original.

*   *   *   *

"These are the heroes that despise the Dutch
And rail at new-come foreigners so much;
Forgetting that themselves are all derived
From the most scoundrel race that ever lived;
A horrid crowd of rambling thieves and drones,
Who ransacked kingdoms and dispeopled towns;
The Pict and painted Briton, treacherous Scot,
By hunger, theft, and rapine hither brought;
Norwegian pirates, buccaneering Danes,
Whose red-haired offspring everywhere remains;
Who joined with Norman-French compound the breed
From whence your true-born Englishmen proceed.

"And lest, by length of time, it be pretended,
The climate may this modern breed have mended,
Wise Providence, to keep us where we are,
Mixes us daily with exceeding care;
We have been Europe's sink, the jakes where she
Voids all her offal outcast progeny;
From our fifth Henry's time the strolling bands
Of banished fugitives from neighbouring lands
Have here a certain sanctuary found:
The eternal refuge of the vagabond,
Wherein but half a common age of time,
Borrowing new blood and manners from the clime,
Proudly they learn all mankind to contemn,
And all their race are true-born Englishmen."

As may be judged from this specimen, there is little
delicacy in Defoe's satire. The lines run on from

beginning to end in the same strain of bold, broad, hearty
banter, as if the whole piece had been written off at a
heat.   The mob did not lynch the audacious humourist.
In the very height of their fury against foreigners, they
stopped short to laugh at themselves.   They were tickled
by the hard blows as we may suppose a rhinoceros to be
tickled by the strokes of an oaken cudgel.   Defoe suddenly woke to find himself the hero of the hour, at least
with the London populace.   The pamphlet was pirated,
and eighty thousand copies, according to his own calculation, were sold in the streets.   Henceforth he described
himself in his title-pages as the author of the *True-Born
Englishman*, and frequently did himself the honour of
quoting from the work as from a well-established classic.
It was also, he has told us, the means of his becoming
personally known to the King, whom he had hitherto
served from a distance.

Defoe was not the man to be abashed by his own
popularity.   He gloried in it, and added to his reputation by taking a prominent part in the proceedings
connected with the famous Kentish Petition, which
marked the turn of the tide in favour of the King's
foreign policy.   Defoe was said to be the author of
" Legion's Memorial " to the House of Commons,
sternly warning the representatives of the freeholders
that they had exceeded their powers in imprisoning the
men who had prayed them to "turn their loyal addresses into Bills of Supply."   When the Kentish
Petitioners were liberated from the custody of the
Sergeant-at-Arms, and feasted by the citizens at Mer-
cers' Hall, Defoe was seated next to them as an
honoured guest.

Unfortunately for Defoe, William did not live long

after he had been honoured with his Majesty's confidence. He declared afterwards that he had often been privately consulted by the King. The pamphlets which he wrote during the close of the reign are all such as might have been directly inspired. That on the Succession is chiefly memorable as containing a suggestion that the heirs of the Duke of Monmouth should be heard as to King Charles's alleged marriage with Lucy Walters. It is possible that this idea may have been sanctioned by the King, who had had painful experience of the disadvantages attending a ruler of foreign extraction, and besides had reason to doubt the attachment of the Princess Sophia to the Protestant faith. When the passionate aversion to war in the popular mind was suddenly changed by the recognition of the Pretender into an equally passionate thirst for it, and the King seized the opportunity to dissolve Parliament and get a new House in accord with the altered temper of the people, Defoe justified the appeal to the freeholders by an examination and assertion of "the Original Power of the Collective Body of the People of England." His last service to the King was a pamphlet bearing the paradoxical title, *Reasons against a War with France.* As Defoe had for nearly a year been zealously working the public mind to a warlike pitch, this title is at first surprising, but the surprise disappears when we find that the pamphlet is an ingenious plea for beginning with a declaration of war against Spain, showing that not only was there just cause for such a war, but that it would be extremely profitable, inasmuch as it would afford occasion for plundering the Spaniards in the West Indies, and thereby making up for whatever losses our trade might suffer from the

French privateers.   And it was more than a mere
plundering descent that Defoe had in view; his object
was that England should take actual possession of the
Spanish Indies, and so rob Spain of its chief source of
wealth.   There was a most powerful buccaneering spirit
concealed under the peaceful title of this pamphlet.
The trick of arresting attention by an unexpected
thesis, such as this promise of reasons for peace when
everybody was dreaming of war, is an art in which
Defoe has never been surpassed.   As we shall have
occasion to see, he practised it more than once too often
for his comfort.

CHAPTER III.

FROM the death of the King in March, 1702, we must date a change in Defoe's relations with the ruling powers. Under William, his position as a political writer had been distinct and honourable. He supported William's policy warmly and straightforwardly, whether he divined it by his own judgment, or learned it by direct or indirect instructions or hints. When charged with writing for a place, he indignantly denied that he held either place or pension at Court, but at another time he admitted that he had been employed by the King and rewarded by him beyond his deserts. Any reward that he received for his literary services was well earned, and there was nothing dishonourable in accepting it. For concealing the connexion while the King was alive, he might plead the custom of the time. But in the confusion of parties and the uncertainty of government that followed William's death, Defoe slid into practices which cannot be justified by any standard of morality.

It was by accident that Defoe drifted into this equivocal position. His first writings under the new reign were in staunch consistency with what he had written

before. He did not try to flatter the Queen as many
others did by slighting her predecessors; on the contrary, he wrote a poem called *The Mock Mourners*, in
which he extolled "the glorious memory"—a phrase
which he did much to bring into use—and charged
those who spoke disrespectfully of William with the
vilest insolence and ingratitude. He sang the praises
of the Queen also, but as he based his joy at her accession on an assurance that she would follow in William's
footsteps, the compliment might be construed as an
exhortation. Shortly afterwards, in another poem, *The
Spanish Descent*, he took his revenge upon the fleet for
not carrying out his West Indian scheme by ridiculing
unmercifully their first fruitless cruise on the Spanish
coast, taking care at the same time to exult in the capture of the galleons at Vigo. In yet another poem—
the success of the *True Born Englishman* seems to have
misguided him into the belief that he had a genius for
verse—he reverted to the Reformation of Manners, and
angered the Dissenters by belabouring certain magis-
trates of their denomination. A pamphlet entitled
A New Test of the Church of England's Loyalty—in which
he twitted the High Church party with being neither
more nor less loyal than the Dissenters, inasmuch as they
consented to the deposition of James and acquiesced
in the accession of Anne—was better received by his
co-religionists.

But when the Bill to prevent occasional conformity
was introduced by some hot-headed partisans of the
High Church, towards the close of 1702, with the
Queen's warm approval, Defoe took a course which
made the Dissenters threaten to cast him altogether
out of the synagogue. We have already seen how

Defoe had taken the lead in attacking the practice of occasional conformity. While his co-religionists were imprecating him as the man who had brought this persecution upon them, Defoe added to their ill-feeling by issuing a jaunty pamphlet in which he proved with provoking unanswerableness that all honest Dissenters were noways concerned in the Bill. Nobody, he said, with his usual bright audacity, but himself "who was altogether born in sin," saw the true scope of the measure. "All those people who designed the Act as a blow to the Dissenting interests in England are mistaken. All those who take it as a prelude or introduction to the further suppressing of the Dissenters, and a step to repealing the Toleration, or intend it as such, are mistaken. . . . . All those phlegmatic Dissenters who fancy themselves undone, and that persecution and desolation is at the door again, are mistaken. All those Dissenters who are really at all disturbed at it, either as an advantage gained by their enemies or as a real disaster upon themselves, are mistaken. All those Dissenters who deprecate it as a judgment, or would vote against it as such if it were in their power, are mistaken." In short, though he did not suppose that the movers of the Bill "did it in mere kindness to the Dissenters, in order to refine and purge them from the scandals which some people had brought upon them," nevertheless it was calculated to effect this object. The Dissenter being a man that was "something desirous of going to Heaven," ventured the displeasure of the civil magistrate at the command of his conscience, which warned him that there were things in the Established form of worship not agreeable to the Will of God as revealed in Scripture. There is nothing in

the Act to the prejudice of this Dissenter; it affects
only the Politic Dissenter, or State Dissenter, who if he
can attend the Established worship without offending
his conscience, has no cause to be a Dissenter.   An Act
against occasional conformity would rid the Dissenting
body of these lukewarm members, and the riddance
would be a good thing for all parties.

It may have been that this cheerful argument, the
legitimate development of Defoe's former writings on
the subject, was intended to comfort his co-religionists
at a moment when the passing of the Act seemed certain. They did not view it in that light; they resented
it bitterly, as an insult in the hour of their misfortune
from the man who had shown their enemies where to
strike. When, however, the Bill, after passing the
Commons, was opposed and modified by the Lords,
Defoe suddenly appeared on a new tack, publishing the
most famous of his political pamphlets, *The Shortest
Way with the Dissenters*, which has, by a strange freak
of circumstances, gained him the honour of being en-
shrined as one of the martyrs of Dissent.   In the
" brief explanation " of the pamphlet which he gave
afterwards, he declared that it had no bearing whatever
upon the Occasional Conformity Bill, pointing to his
former writings on the subject, in which he had denounced the practice, and welcomed the Bill as a useful
instrument for purging the Dissenting bodies of half-
and-half professors.   It was intended, he said, as a
banter upon the High-flying Tory Churchmen, putting into plain English the drift of their furious invec-
tives against the Dissenters, and so, " by an irony not
unusual," answering them out of their own mouths.

The *Shortest Way* is sometimes spoken of as a piece

of exquisite irony, and on the other hand Mr. Saints-
bury[1] has raised the question whether the representation of an extreme case, in which the veil is never lifted
from the writer's own opinions, can properly be called
irony at all. This last is, perhaps, a question belonging to the strict definition of the figures of speech; but,
however that might be settled, it is a mistake to de-
scribe Defoe's art in this pamphlet as delicate. There
are no subtle strokes of wit in it such as we find in
some of Swift's ironical pieces. Incomparably more
effective as an engine of controversy, it is not entitled
to the same rank as a literary exercise. Its whole merit
and its rousing political force lay in the dramatic genius
with which Defoe personated the temper of a thoroughgoing High-flier. putting into plain and spirited English
such sentiments as a violent partisan would not dare to
utter except in the unguarded heat of familiar discourse,
or the half-humorous ferocity of intoxication. Have
done, he said, addressing the Dissenters, with this cackle
about Peace and Union, and the Christian duties of
moderation, which you raise now that you find "your
day is over, your power gone, and the throne of this
nation possessed by a Royal, English, true, and ever-
constant member of and friend to the Church of England. . . We have heard none of this lesson for fourteen
years past. We have been huffed and bullied with your
Act of Toleration; you have told us that you are the
Church established by law as well as others; have set
up your canting synagogues at our Church doors, and
the Church and members have been loaded with reproaches, with oaths, associations, abjurations, and what

[1] In an admirable article on Defoe in the *Encyclopædia
Britannica*.

not. Where has been the mercy, the forbearance, the
charity, you have shown to tender consciences of the
Church of England, that could not take oaths as fast
as you made them; that having sworn allegiance to
their lawful and rightful King, could not dispense with
that oath, their King being still alive, and swear to your
new hodge-podge of a Dutch constitution ? . . . Now
that the tables are turned upon you, you must not be
persecuted; 'tis not a Christian spirit." You talk of
persecution ; what persecution have you to complain of ?
"The first execution of the laws against Dissenters in
England was in the days of King James I. And what
did it amount to ? Truly the worst they suffered was
at their own request to let them go to New England and
erect a new colony, and give them great privileges,
grants, and suitable powers, keep them under protection, and defend them against all invaders, and receive
no taxes or revenue from them. This was the cruelty
of the Church of England, fatal lenity ! 'Twas the ruin
of that excellent prince, King Charles I. Had King
James sent all the Puritans in England away to the
West Indies, we had been a national, unmixed Church ;
the Church of England had been kept undivided and
entire. To requite the lenity of the father, they take up
arms against the son ; conquer, pursue, take, imprison,
and at last put to death the Anointed of God, and destroy the very being and nature of government, setting up
a sordid impostor, who had neither title to govern, nor
understanding to manage, but supplied that want with
power, bloody and desperate councils, and craft, without
conscience." How leniently had King Charles treated
these barbarous regicides, coming in all mercy and love,
cherishing them, preferring them, giving them employ-

ment in his service. As for King James, "as if mercy
was the inherent quality of the family, he began his
reign with unusual favour to them, nor could their
joining with the Duke of Monmouth against him move
him to do himself justice upon them, but that mistaken
prince thought to win them by gentleness and love, proclaimed a universal liberty to them, and rather discoun-
tenanced the Church of England than them. How they
requited him all the world knows."   Under King
William, "a king of their own," they "crope into all
places of trust and profit," engrossed the ministry, and
insulted the Church. But they must not expect this
kind of thing to continue. "No, gentlemen, the time
of mercy is past; your day of grace is over; you should
have practised peace, and moderation, and charity, if you
expected any yourselves."

In this heroic strain the pamphlet proceeds, reaching
at length the suggestion that "if one severe law were
made, and punctually executed, that whoever was found
at a conventicle should be banished the nation, and the
preacher be hanged, we should soon see an end of the
tale—they would all come to church, and one age would
make us all one again." That was the mock church-
man's shortest way for the suppression of Dissent.
He supported his argument by referring to the success
with which Louis XIV. had put down the Huguenots.
There was no good in half-measures, fines of five shillings a month for not coming to the Sacrament, and one
shilling a week for not coming to church. It was vain
to expect compliance from such trifling. "The light
foolish handling of them by mulcts, fines, etc., 'tis their
glory and their advantage. If the gallows instead of
the counter, and the galleys instead of the fines, were

the reward of going to a conventicle, to preach or hear,
there would not be so many sufferers—the spirit of
martyrdom is over. They that will go to church to be
chosen sheriffs and mayors, would go to forty churches
rather than be hanged." "Now let us crucify the
thieves," said the author of this truculent advice in
conclusion. "And may God Almighty put it into the
hearts of all friends of truth to lift up a standard
against pride and Antichrist, that the posterity of the
sons of error may be rooted out from the face of this
land for ever."

Defoe's disguise was so complete, his caricature of the
ferocious High-flier so near to life, that at first people
doubted whether the *Shortest Way* was the work of a satirist or a fanatic. When the truth leaked out, as it soon
did, the Dissenters were hardly better pleased than while
they feared that the proposal was serious. With the
natural timidity of precariously situated minorities,
they could not enter into the humour of it. The very
title was enough to make them shrink and tremble.
The only people who were really in a position to enjoy
the jest were the Whigs. The High Churchmen, some
of whom, it is said, were at first so far taken in as to
express their warm approval, were furious when they
discovered the trick that had been played upon them.
The Tory ministers of the Queen felt themselves bound
to take proceedings against the author, whose identity
seems to have soon become an open secret. Learning
this, Defoe went into concealment. A proclamation offering a reward for his discovery was advertised in the *Gazette*. The description of the fugitive
is interesting ; it is the only extant record of
Defoe's personal appearance, except the portrait pre-

fixed to his collected works, in which the mole is faithfully reproduced :—

"He is a middle-aged, spare man, about forty years old, of
a brown complexion, and dark-brown coloured hair, but wears
a wig ; a hooked nose, a sharp chin, grey eyes, and a large
mole near his mouth: was born in London, and for many
years was a hose-factor in Freeman's Yard in Cornhill, and
now is the owner of the brick and pantile works near Tilbury
Fort in Essex."

This advertisement was issued on the 10th of January,
1703. Meantime the printer and the publisher were
seized. From his safe hiding, Defoe put forth an explanation, protesting, as we have seen, that his pamphlet
had not the least retrospect to or concern in the public
bills in Parliament now depending, or any other proceeding of either House or of the Government relating
to the Dissenters, whose occasional conformity the author
has constantly opposed. It was merely, he pleaded,
the cant of the Non-juring party exposed ; and he
mentioned several printed books in which the same
objects were expressed, though not in words so plain,
and at length. But the Government would not take
this view ; he had represented virulent partisans as
being supreme in the Queen's counsels, and his design
was manifest " to blacken the Church party as men of
a persecuting spirit, and to prepare the mob for what
further service he had for them to do." Finding that
they would not listen to him, Defoe surrendered himself,
in order that others might not suffer for his offence.
He was indicted on the 24th of February. On the 25th,
the *Shortest Way* was brought under the notice of the
House of Commons, and ordered to be burnt by the
common hangman. His trial came on in July. He

was found guilty of a seditious libel, and sentenced
to pay a fine of 200 marks to the Queen, stand three
times in the pillory, be imprisoned during the Queen's
pleasure, and find sureties for his good behaviour
for seven years.

Defoe complained that three Dissenting ministers,
whose poor he had fed in the days of his prosperity,
had refused to visit him during his confinement in
Newgate. There was, doubtless, a want of charity in
their action, but there was also a want of honesty in
his complaint. If he applied for their spiritual minis-
trations, they had considerable reason for treating his
application as a piece of provoking effrontery. Though
Defoe was in prison for this banter upon the High-
fliers, it is a mistake to regard him as a martyr, except
by accident, to the cause of Toleration as we understand
it now, and as the Dissenters bore the brunt of the
battle for it then. Before his trial and conviction,
while he lay in prison, he issued an exposition of his
views of a fair Toleration in a tract entitled *The Shortest
Way to Peace and Union*. The toleration which he
advised, and which commended itself to the moderate
Whigs with whom he had acted under King William
and was probably acting now, was a purely spiritual
Toleration. His proposal, in fact, was identical with
that of Charles Leslie's in the *New Association*, one of
the pamphlets which he professed to take off in his
famous squib. Leslie had proposed that the Dissenters
should be excluded from all civil employments, and
should be forced to remain content with liberty of
worship. Addressing the Dissenters, Defoe, in effect,
urged them to anticipate forcible exclusion by voluntary
withdrawal. Extremes on both sides should be in-

dustriously crushed and discouraged, and the extremes
on the Dissenting side were those who not being content
to worship after their own fashion, had also a hankering
after the public service.   It is the true interest of the
Dissenters in England, Defoe argued, to be governed
by a Church of England magistracy ; and with his usual
paradoxical hardihood, he told his co-religionists bluntly
that "the first reason of his proposition was that they
were not qualified to be trusted with the government of
themselves."   When we consider the active part Defoe
himself took in public affairs, we shall not be surprised
that offence was given by his countenancing the civil
disabilities of Dissenters, and that the Dissenting
preachers declined to recognise him as properly belonging to their body.   It was not, indeed, as a Dissenter
that Defoe was prosecuted by the violent Tories then in
power, but as the suspected literary instrument of the
great Whig leaders.

This, of course, in no way diminishes the harsh and
spiteful impolicy of the sentence passed on Defoe.
Its terms were duly put in execution.   The offending
satirist stood in the pillory on the three last days of
July, 1703, before the Royal Exchange in Cornhill, near
the Conduit in Cheapside, and at Temple Bar.   It is
incorrect, however, to say with Pope that

"Earless on high stood unabashed Defoe."

His ears were not cropped, as the barbarous phrase
went, and he had no reason to be abashed.   His reception by the mob was very different from that accorded
to the anti-Jacobite Fuller, a scurrilous rogue who had
tried to make a few pounds by a Plain Proof that

the Chevalier was a supposititious child. The author of the *True-Born Englishman* was a popular favourite, and his exhibition in the pillory was an occasion of triumph and not of ignominy to him. A ring of admirers was formed round the place of punishment, and bunches of flowers instead of handfuls of garbage were thrown at the criminal. Tankards of ale and stoups of wine were drunk in his honour by the multitude whom he had delighted with his racy verse and charmed by his bold defiance of the authorities.

The enthusiasm was increased by the timely publication of a *Hymn to the Pillory*, in which Defoe boldly declared the iniquity of his sentence, and pointed out to the Government more proper objects of their severity. Atheists ought to stand there, he said, profligate beaux, swindling stock-jobbers, fanatic Jacobites, and the commanders who had brought the English fleet into disgrace. As for him, his only fault lay in his not being understood; but he was perhaps justly punished for being such a fool as to trust his meaning to irony. It would seem that though the Government had committed Defoe to Newgate, they did not dare, even before the manifestation of popular feeling in his favour, to treat him as a common prisoner. He not only had liberty to write, but he found means to convey his manuscripts to the printer. Of these privileges he had availed himself with that indomitable energy and fertility of resource which we find reason to admire at every stage in his career, and most of all now that he was in straits. In the short interval between his arrest and his conviction he carried on a vigorous warfare with both hands,—with one hand seeking to propitiate the Government, with the other attracting support outside among the people. He

proved to the Government incontestably by a collection
of his writings that he was a man of moderate views,
who had no aversion in principle even to the proposals
of the *New Association*. He proved the same thing to
the people at large by publishing this *Collection of the
writings of the author of the True-Born Englishman*, but
he accompanied the proof by a lively appeal to their
sympathy under the title of *More Reformation, a Satire
on himself*, a lament over his own folly which was
calculated to bring pressure on the Government against
prosecuting a man so innocent of public wrong. When,
in spite of his efforts, a conviction was recorded against
him, he adopted a more defiant tone towards the Government. He wrote the *Hymn to the Pillory*. This daring
effusion was hawked in the streets among the crowd that
had assembled to witness his penance in the

> "hieroglyphic State-machine,
> Contrived to punish Fancy in."

"Come," he cried, in the concluding lines—

> "Tell 'em the M—— that placed him here
> Are Sc——ls to the times,
> Are at a loss to find his guilt,
> And can't commit his crimes."

"M——" stands for Men, and "Sc——ls" for Scandals.
Defoe delighted in this odd use of methods of reserve,
more common in his time than in ours.

The dauntless courage of Defoe's *Hymn to the Pillory*
can only be properly appreciated, when we remember
with what savage outrage it was the custom of the mob
to treat those who were thus exposed to make a London
holiday.   From the pillory he was taken back to

Newgate, there to be imprisoned during her Majesty's pleasure. His confinement must have been much less disagreeable to him than it would have been to one of less hardy temperament. Defoe was not the man to shrink with loathing from the companionship of thieves, highwaymen, forgers, coiners, and pirates. Curiosity was a much stronger power with him than disgust. Newgate had something of the charm for Defoe that a hospital full of hideous diseases has for an enthusiastic surgeon. He spent many pleasant hours in listening to the tales of his adventurous fellow-prisoners. Besides, the Government did not dare to deprive him of the liberty of writing and publishing. This privilege enabled him to appeal to the public, whose ear he had gained in the character of an undismayed martyr, an enjoyment which to so buoyant a man must have compensated for a great deal of irksome suffering. He attributed the failure of his pantile works at Tilbury to his removal from the management of them; but bearing in mind the amount of success that had attended his efforts when he was free, it is fair to suppose that he was not altogether sorry for the excuse. It was by no means the intention of his High Church persecutors that Defoe should enjoy himself in Newgate, and he himself lamented loudly the strange reverse by which he had passed within a few months from the closet of a king to a prisoner's cell; but on the whole he was probably as happy in Newgate as he had been at Whitehall. His wife and six children were most to be commiserated, and their distress was his heaviest trial.

The first use which Defoe made of his pen after his exhibition in the pillory was to reply to a Dissenting minister who had justified the practice of occasional

conformity.   He thereby marked once more his separa-
tion from the extreme Dissenters, who were struggling
against having their religion made a disqualification for
offices of public trust.   But in the changes of parties at
Court he soon found a reason for marking his separation
from the opposite extreme, and facing the other way.
Under the influence of the moderate Tories, Marlborough,
Godolphin, and their invaluable ally, the Duchess, the
Queen was gradually losing faith in the violent Tories.
According to Swift, she began to dislike her bosom
friend, Mrs. Freeman, from the moment of her accession, but though she may have chafed under the yoke
of her favourite, she could not at once shake off the
domination of that imperious will.   The Duchess, finding
the extreme Tories unfavourable to the war in which
her husband's honour and interests were deeply engaged,
became a hot partisan against them, and used all their
blunders to break down their power at Court.   Day by
day she impressed upon the Queen the necessity of peace
and union at home in the face of the troubles abroad.
The moderate men of both parties must be rallied round
the throne.   Extremes on both sides must be discouraged.
Spies were set to work to take note of such rash expressions among "the hot and angry men" as would be
likely to damage them in the Queen's favour.   Queen
Anne had not a little of the quiet tenacity and spiteful-
ness of enfeebled constitutions, but in the end reason
prevailed, resentment at importunity was overcome,
and the hold of the High Churchmen on her affections
gave way.

Nobody, Swift has told us, could better disguise her
feelings than the Queen.   The first intimation which
the High Church party had of her change of views was

her opening speech to Parliament on the 9th November, 1703, in which she earnestly desired parties in both Houses to avoid heats and divisions. Defoe at once threw himself in front of the rising tide. Whether he divined for himself that the influence of the Earl of Nottingham, the Secretary of State, to whom he owed his prosecution and imprisonment, was waning, or obtained a hint to that effect from his Whig friends, we do not know, but he lost no time in issuing from his prison a bold attack upon the High Churchmen. In his *Challenge of Peace, addressed to the whole Nation*, he denounced them as Church Vultures and Ecclesiastical Harpies. It was they and not the Dissenters that were the prime movers of strife and dissension. How are peace and union to be obtained, he asks. He will show people first how peace and union cannot be obtained.

"First, Sacheverell's Bloody Flag of Defiance is not the way to Peace and Union. *The shortest way to destroy is not the shortest way to unite.* Persecution, Laws to Compel, Restrain, or force the Conscience of one another, is not the way to this Union, which her Majesty has so earnestly recommended.

"Secondly, to repeal or contract the late Act of Toleration is not the way for this so much wished-for happiness; to have laws revived that should set one party a plundering, excommunicating and unchurching another, that should renew the oppressions and devastations of late reigns, this will not by any means contribute to this Peace, which all good men desire.

"New Associations and proposals to divest men of their freehold right for differences in opinion, and take away the right of Dissenters voting in elections of Members; this is not the way to Peace and Union.

"Railing pamphlets, buffooning our brethren as a party to be suppressed, and dressing them up in the Bear's skin for all

the dogs in the street to bait them, is not the way to Peace
and Union.

"Railing sermons, exciting people to hatred and contempt
of their brethren, because they differ in opinions, is not the
way to Peace and Union.

"Shutting all people out of employment and the service
of their Prince and Country, unless they can comply with
indifferent ceremonies of religion, is far from the way to
Peace and Union.

"Reproaching the Succession settled by Parliament, and
reviving the abdicated title of the late King James, and
his supposed family, cannot tend to this Peace and Union.

"Laws against Occasional Conformity, and compelling
people who bear offices to a total conformity, and yet force
them to take and serve in those public employments, cannot
contribute to this Peace and Union."

In this passage Defoe seems to ally himself more
closely with his Dissenting brethren than he had done
before. It was difficult for him, with his published views
on the objectionableness of occasional conformity, and
the propriety of Dissenters leaving the magistracy in
the hands of the Church, to maintain his new position
without incurring the charge of inconsistency. The
charge was freely made, and his own writings were
collected as a testimony against him, but he met the
charge boldly. The Dissenters ought not to practise
occasional conformity, but if they could reconcile it
with their consciences, they ought not to receive tem-
poral punishment for practising it. The Dissenters
ought to withdraw from the magistracy, but it was
persecution to exclude them. In tract after tract of
brilliant and trenchant argument, he upheld these views,
with his usual courage attacking most fiercely those
antagonists who went most nearly on the lines of his
own previous writings. Ignoring what he had said

before, he now proved clearly that the Occasional Conformity Bill was a breach of the Act of Toleration.
There was little difference between his own *Shortest Way
to Peace and Union* and Sir Humphrey Mackworth's
Peace at Home, but he assailed the latter pamphlet
vigorously, and showed that it had been the practice in
all countries for Dissenters from the established religion
to have a share in the business of the State. At the
same time he never departed so far from the "moderate"
point of view, as to insist that Dissenters ought to be
admitted to a share in the business of the State. Let
the High Church ministers be dismissed, and moderate
men summoned to the Queen's councils, and the Dissenters would have every reason to be content. They
would acquiesce with pleasure in a ministry and magistracy of Low Churchmen.

Defoe's assaults upon the High Church Tories were
neither interdicted nor resented by the Government,
though he lay in prison at their mercy. Throughout
the winter of 1703-4 the extreme members of the
Ministry, though they had still a majority in the House
of Commons, felt the Queen's coldness increase. Their
former high place in her regard and their continued
hold upon Parliament tempted them to assume airs
of independence which gave deeper offence than her
unruffled courtesy led either them or their rivals to
suspect. At last the crisis came. The Earl of Nottingham took the rash step of threatening to resign unless
the Whig Dukes of Somerset and Devonshire were
dismissed from the Cabinet. To his surprise and chagrin,
his resignation was accepted (1704), and two more of his
party were dismissed from office at the same time.

The successor of Nottingham was Robert Harley, afterwards created Earl of Oxford and Mortimer. He gave evidence late in life of his love for literature by forming the collection of manuscripts known as the Harleian, and we know from Swift that he was deeply impressed with the importance of having allies in the Press. He entered upon office in May, 1704, and one of his first acts was to convey to Defoe the message, "Pray, ask that gentleman what I can do for him." Defoe replied by likening himself to the blind man in the parable, and paraphrasing his prayer, "Lord, that I may receive my sight!" He would not seem to have obtained his liberty immediately, but, through Harley's influence, he was set free towards the end of July or the beginning of August. The Queen also, he afterwards said, "was pleased particularly to inquire into his circumstances and family, and by Lord Treasurer Godolphin to send a considerable supply to his wife and family, and to send him to the prison money to pay his fine and the expenses of his discharge."

On what condition was Defoe released? On condition, according to the *Elegy on the Author of the True-Born Englishman*, which he published immediately after his discharge, that he should keep silence for seven years, or at least "not write what some people might not like." To the public he represented himself as a martyr grudgingly released by the Government, and restrained from attacking them only by his own bond and the fear of legal penalties.

> " Memento Mori here I stand,
>   With silent lips but speaking hand ;
>   A walking shadow of a Poet,
>   But bound to hold my tongue and never show it.
>   A monument of injury,
>   A sacrifice to legal t(yrann)y."

"For shame, gentlemen," he humorously cries to his enemies, "do not strike a dead man ; beware, scribblers, of fathering your pasquinades against authority upon me ; for seven years the True-Born Englishman is tied under sureties and penalties not to write.

> "To seven long years of silence I betake,
> Perhaps by then I may forget to speak."

This elegy he has been permitted to publish as his last speech and dying confession—

> "When malefactors come to die
> They claim uncommon liberty :
> Freedom of speech gives no distaste,
> They let them talk at large, because they talk their last."

The public could hardly have supposed from this what Defoe afterwards admitted to have been the true state of the case, namely, that on leaving prison he was taken into the service of the Government. He obtained an appointment, that is to say a pension, from the Queen, and was employed on secret services. When charged afterwards with having written by Harley's instructions, he denied this, but admitted the existence of certain "capitulations," in which he stipulated for liberty to write according to his own judgment, guided only by a sense of gratitude to his benefactor. There is reason to believe that even this is not the whole truth. Documents which Mr. Lee recently brought to light make one suspect that Defoe was all the time in private relations with the leaders of the Whig party. Of this more falls to be said in another place. The True-Born Englishman was, indeed, dead. Defoe was no longer the straightforward advocate of King William's policy. He was engaged henceforward in serving two masters, persuading each that he served him alone, and persuading the public, in spite of numberless insinuations, that he served nobody but them and himself, and wrote simply as a free lance under the jealous sufferance of the Government of the day.

I must reserve for a separate chapter some account of Defoe's greatest political work, which he began while he still lay in Newgate, the *Review*. Another work which he wrote and published at the same period deserves attention on different grounds. His history of the great storm of November 1703, *A Collection of the most remarkable Casualties and Disasters which happened in the late Dreadful Tempest, both by Sea and Land*, may be set down as the first of his works of invention. It is a most minute and circumstantial record, containing many letters from eye-witnesses of what happened in their immediate neighbourhood. Defoe could have seen little of the storm himself from the interior of Newgate, but it is possible that the letters are genuine, and that he compiled other details from published accounts. Still, we are justified in suspecting that his annals of the storm are no more authentic history than his *Journal of the Plague*, or his *Memoirs of a Cavalier*, and that for many of the incidents he is equally indebted to his imagination.

CHAPTER IV.

It was a bold undertaking for a prisoner in Newgate to engage to furnish a newspaper written wholly by himself, "purged from the errors and partiality of newswriters and petty statesmen of all sides." It would, of course, have been an impossible undertaking if the *Review* had been, either in size or in contents, like a newspaper of the present time. The *Review* was, in its first stage, a sheet of eight small quarto pages. After the first two numbers, it was reduced in size to four pages, but a smaller type was used, so that the amount of matter remained nearly the same—about equal in bulk to two modern leading articles. At first the issue was weekly; after four numbers it became bi-weekly, and so remained for a year.

For the character of the *Review* it is difficult to find a parallel. There was nothing like it at the time, and nothing exactly like it has been attempted since. The nearest approach to it among its predecessors was the *Observator*, a small weekly journal written by the erratic John Tutchin, in which passing topics, political and social, were discussed in dialogues. Personal scandals were a prominent feature in the *Observator*. Defoe was not insensible to the value of this element to a popular journal. He knew, he said, that people liked to be amused; and he supplied this want in a section of his paper entitled " Mercure Scandale ; or Advice from the Scandalous Club, being a weekly history of Nonsense, Impertinence, Vice, and Debauchery." Under this attractive heading, Defoe noticed current scandals, his club being represented as a tribunal before which offenders were brought, their cases heard, and sentence passed upon them. Slanderers of the True-Born Englishman frequently figure in its proceedings. It was in this section also that Defoe exposed the errors of contemporary news-writers, the *Postman*, the *Post-Boy*, the *London Post*, the *Flying Post*, and the *Daily Courant*. He could not in his prison pretend to superior information regarding the events of the day; the errors which he exposed were chiefly blunders in geography and history. The Mercure Scandale was avowedly intended to amuse the frivolous. The lapse of time has made its artificial sprightliness dreary. It was in the serious portion of the *Review*, the Review proper, that Defoe showed most of his genius. The design of this was nothing less than to give a true picture, drawn with " an impartial and exact historical pen," of the domestic and foreign affairs of all the States of Europe. It was essential, he thought, that at such a time of commotion Englishmen should be thoroughly informed of the strength and the political interests and proclivities of the various European Powers. He could not undertake to tell his readers what was passing from day to day, but he could explain to them the policy of the Continental Courts ; he could show how that policy was affected by their past history

and present interests ; he could calculate the forces at
their disposal, set forth the grounds of their alliances,
and generally put people in a position to follow the
great game that was being played on the European
chess-board.   In the *Review*, in fact, as he himself
described his task, he was writing a history sheet by
sheet, and letting the world see it as it went on.

This excellent plan of instruction was carried out
with incomparable brilliancy of method, and vivacity
of style.   Defoe was thoroughly master of his subject;
he had read every history that he could lay his hands
on, and his connexion with King William had guided
him to the mainsprings of political action, and fixed in
his mind clear principles for England's foreign policy.
Such a mass of facts and such a maze of interests would
have encumbered and perplexed a more commonplace
intellect, but Defoe handled them with experienced and
buoyant ease.   He had many arts for exciting attention.   His confinement in Newgate, from which the first
number of the *Review* was issued on the 19th February,
1704, had in no way impaired his clear-sighted daring
and self-confident skill.   There was a sparkle of paradox
and a significant lesson in the very title of his journal
—*A Review of the Affairs of France.*   When, by
and by, he digressed to the affairs of Sweden and
Poland, and filled number after number with the
history of Hungary, people kept asking, " What has
this to do with France ? "   " How little you understand
my design," was Defoe's retort.   " Patience till my
work is completed, and then you will see that, however
much I may seem to have been digressing, I have
always kept strictly to the point.   Do not judge me as
you judged St. Paul's before the roof was put on.   It

is not affairs *in* France that I have undertaken to explain, but the affars *of* France, and the affairs of France are the affairs of Europe. So great is the power of the French money, the artifice of their conduct, the terror of their arms, that they can bring the greatest kings in Europe to promote their interest and grandeur at the expense of their own."

Defoe delighted to brave common prejudice by throwing full in its face paradoxes expressed in the most unqualified language. While we were at war with France, and commonplace hunters after popularity were doing their utmost to flatter the national vanity, Defoe boldly announced his intention of setting forth the wonderful greatness of the French nation, the enormous numbers of their armies, the immense wealth of their treasury, the marvellous vigour of their administration. He ridiculed loudly those writers who pretended that we should have no difficulty in beating them, and filled their papers with dismal stories about the poverty and depopulation of the country. "Consider the armies that the French King has raised," cried Defoe, "and the reinforcements and subsidies he has sent to the King of Spain; does that look like a depopulated country and an impoverished exchequer?" It was perhaps a melancholy fact, but what need to apologise for telling the truth? At once, of course, a shout was raised against him for want of patriotism; he was a French pensioner, a Jacobite, a hireling of the Peace-party. This was the opportunity on which the chuckling paradox-monger had counted. He protested that he was not drawing a map of the French power to terrify the English. But, he said, "there are two cheats equally hurtful to us; the first to terrify us, the last to

make us too easy and consequently too secure; 'tis
equally dangerous for us to be terrified into despair and
bullied into more terror of our enemies than we need,
or to be so exalted in conceit of our own force as to
undervalue and contemn the power which we cannot
reduce." To blame him for making clear the greatness
of the French power, was to act as if the Romans had
killed the geese in the Capitol for frightening them out
of their sleep. "If I, like an honest Protestant goose,
have gaggled too loud of the French power, and raised
the country, the French indeed may have reason to cut
my throat if they could; but 'tis hard my own countrymen, to whom I have shown their danger, and whom I
have endeavoured to wake out of their sleep, should
take offence at the timely discovery."

If we open the first volume, or indeed any volume of
the *Review*, at random, we are almost certain to meet
with some electric shock of paradox designed to arouse
the attention of the torpid. In one number we find
the writer, ever daring and alert, setting out with an
eulogium on "the wonderful benefit of arbitrary power"
in France. He runs on in this vein for some time, accu-
mulating examples of the wonderful benefit, till the patience of his liberty-loving readers is sufficiently exaspe-
rated, and then he turns round with a grin of mockery
and explains that he means benefit to the monarch, not to
the subject. "If any man ask me what are the benefits
of arbitrary power to the subject, I answer these two,
poverty and *subjection*." But to an ambitious monarch
unlimited power is a necessity; unless he can count
upon instant obedience to his will, he only courts defeat
if he embarks in schemes of aggression and conquest.

" When a Prince must court his subjects to give him leave
to raise an army, and when that's done, tell him when he
must disband them ; that if he wants money, he must assemble
the States of his country, and not only give them good words
to get it, and tell them what 'tis for, but give them an
account how it is expended before he asks for more. The
subjects in such a government are certainly happy in having
their property and privileges secured, but if I were of his
Privy Council, I would advise such a Prince to content himself within the compass of his own government, and never
think of invading his neighbours or increasing his dominions,
for subjects who stipulate with their Princes, and make conditions of government, who claim to be governed by laws and
make those laws themselves, who need not pay their money
but when they see cause, and may refuse to pay it when
demanded without their consent ; such subjects will never
empty their purses upon foreign wars for enlarging the glory
of their sovereign."

This glory he describes as "the leaf-gold which the
devil has laid over the backside of ambition, to make it
glitter to the world."

Defoe's knowledge of the irritation caused among the
Dissenters by his *Shortest Way*, did not prevent him
from shocking them and annoying the high Tories by
similar *jeux d'esprit*. He had no tenderness for the
feelings of such of his brethren as had not his own
robust sense of humour and boyish glee in the free
handling of dangerous weapons. Thus we find him,
among his eulogies of the Grand Monarque, particularly
extolling him for the revocation of the Edict of Nantes.
By the expulsion of the Protestants, Louis impoverished
and unpeopled part of his country, but it was "the
most politic action the French King ever did." "I
don't think fit to engage here in a dispute about the
honesty of it," says Defoe ; "but till he had first

cleared the country of that numerous injured people,
he could never have ventured to carry an offensive war
into all the borders of Europe." And Defoe was not
content with shocking the feelings of his nominal co-
religionists by a light treatment of matters in which he
agreed with them. He upheld with all his might the
opposite view from theirs on two important questions of
foreign policy. While the Confederates were doing battle
on all sides against France, the King of Sweden was
making war on his own account against Poland for the
avowed purpose of placing a Protestant prince on the
throne. Extreme Protestants in England were disposed
to think that Charles XII. was fighting the Lord's
battle in Poland. But Defoe was strongly of opinion
that the work in which all Protestants ought at that
moment to be engaged was breaking down the power of
France, and as Charles refused to join the Confederacy,
and the Catholic prince against whom he was fighting
was a possible adherent, the ardent preacher of union
among the Protestant powers insisted upon regarding
him as a practical ally of France, and urged that the
English fleet should be sent into the Baltic to inter-
rupt his communications. Disunion among Protestants,
argued Defoe, was the main cause of French greatness ;
if the Swedish King would not join the Confederacy of
his own free will, he should be compelled to join it, or
at least to refrain from weakening it.

Defoe treated the revolt of the Hungarians against the
Emperor with the same regard to the interests of the
Protestant cause. Some uneasiness was felt in England
at co-operating with an ally who so cruelly oppressed
his Protestant subjects, and some scruple of conscience
at seeming to countenance the oppression. Defoe fully

admitted the wrongs of the Hungarians, but argued that this was not the time for them to press their claims for redress. He would not allow that they were justified at such a moment in calling in the aid of the Turks against the Emperor. "It is not enough that a nation be Protestant and the people our friends; if they will join with our enemies, they are Papists, Turks, and Heathens, to us." "If the Protestants in Hungary will make the Protestant religion in Hungary clash with the Protestant religion in all the rest of Europe, we must prefer the major interest to the minor." Defoe treats every foreign question from the cool high-political point of view, generally taking up a position from which he can expose the unreasonableness of both sides. In the case of the Cevennois insurgents, one party had used the argument that it was unlawful to encourage rebellion even among the subjects of a prince with whom we were at war. With this Defoe dealt in one article, proving with quite a superfluity of illustration that we were justified by all the precedents of recent history in sending support to the rebellious subjects of Louis XIV. It was the general custom of Europe to "assist the malcontents of our neighbours." Then in another article he considered whether, being lawful, it was also expedient, and he answered this in the negative, treating with scorn a passionate appeal for the Cevennois entitled "Europe enslaved if the Camisars are not relieved." "What nonsense is this," he cried, "about a poor despicable handful of men who have only made a little diversion in the great war." "The haste these men are in to have that done which they cannot show us the way to do," he cried; and proceeded to prove in a minute discussion of conceivable strategic

movements that it was impossible for us in the circumstances to send the Camisards the least relief.

There is no reference in the *Review* to Defoe's release
from prison. Two numbers a week were issued with the
same punctuality before and after, and there is no per-
ceptible difference either in tone or in plan. Before he
left prison, and before the fall of the high Tory Ministers,
he had thrown in his lot boldly with the moderate men,
and he did not identify himself more closely with any
political section after Harley and Godolphin recognised
the value of his support and gave him liberty and
pecuniary help. In the first number of the *Review* he
had declared his freedom from party ties, and his un-
reserved adherence to truth and the public interest, and
he made frequent protestation of this independence.
"I am not a party man," he kept saying; "at least, I
resolve this shall not be a party paper." In discussing
the affairs of France, he took more than one side-glance
homewards, but always with the protest that he had no
interest to serve but that of his country. The absolute
power of Louis, for example, furnished him with an
occasion for lamenting the disunited counsels of Her
Majesty's Cabinet. Without imitating the despotic
form of the French Government, he said, there are ways
by which we might secure under our own forms greater
decision and promptitude on the part of the Executive.
When Nottingham was dismissed, he rejoiced openly,
not because the ex-Secretary had been his persecutor,
but because at last there was unity of views among the
Queen's Ministers. He joined naturally in the exulta-
tion over Marlborough's successes, but in the *Review*,
and in his *Hymn to Victory*, separately published, he
courteously diverted some part of the credit to the new

Ministry. "Her Majesty's measures, moved by new and polished councils, have been pointed more directly at the root of the French power than ever we have seen before. I hope no man will suppose I reflect on the memory of King William; I know 'tis impossible the Queen should more sincerely wish the reduction of France than his late Majesty; but if it is expected I should say he was not worse served, oftener betrayed, and consequently hurried into more mistakes and disasters, than Her Majesty now is, this must be by somebody who believes I know much less of the public matters of those days than I had the honour to be informed of." But this praise, he represented, was not the praise of a partisan; it was an honest compliment wrung from a man whose only connexion with the Government was a bond for his good behaviour, an undertaking "not to write what some people might not like."

Defoe's hand being against every member of the writing brotherhood, it was natural that his reviews should not pass without severe criticisms. He often complained of the insults, ribaldry, Billingsgate, and Bear-garden language to which he was exposed; and some of his biographers have taken these lamentations seriously, and expressed their regret that so good a man should have been so much persecuted. But as he deliberately provoked these assaults, and never missed a chance of effective retort, it is difficult to sympathise with him on any ground but his manifest delight in the strife of tongues. Infinitely the superior of his antagonists in power, he could affect to treat them with good humour, but this good humour was not easy to reciprocate when combined with an imperturbable assumption that they were all fools or knaves. When we find him, after humbly asking pardon for all his errors of the press, errors of the pen, or errors of opinion, expressing a wish that "all gentlemen on the other side would give him equal occasion to honour them for their charity, temper, and gentlemanlike dealing, as for their learning and virtue," and offering to "capitulate with them, and enter into a treaty or cartel for exchange of good language," we may, if we like, admire his superior mastery of the weapons of irritation, but pity is out of place.

The number of February 17, 1705, was announced by Defoe as being "the last Review of this volume, and designed to be so of this work." But on the following Tuesday, the regular day for the appearance of the *Review*, he issued another number, declaring that he could not quit the volume without some remarks on "charity and poverty." On Saturday yet another last number appeared, dealing with some social subjects which he had been urged by correspondents to discuss. Then on Tuesday, February 27, apologising for the frequent turning of his design, he issued the Preface to a new volume of the *Review* with a slight change of title. He would overtake sooner or later all the particulars of French greatness which he had promised to survey, but as the course of his narrative had brought him to England, and he might stay there for some time, it was as well that this should be indicated in the title, which was henceforth to be A Review of the Affairs of France, with Observations on Affairs at Home. He had intended, he said, to abandon the work altogether, but some gentlemen had prevailed with him to go on, and had promised that he should not be at a loss by it. It was now to be issued three times a week.

CHAPTER V.

In putting forth the prospectus of the second volume of his *Review*, Defoe intimated that its prevailing topic would be the Trade of England—a vast subject, with many branches, all closely interwoven with one another and with the general well-being of the kingdom. It grieved him, he said, to see the nation involved in such evils while remedies lay at hand which blind guides could not, and wicked guides would not, see—trade decaying, yet within reach of the greatest improvements, the navy flourishing yet fearfully mismanaged, rival factions brawling and fighting when they ought to combine for the common good. "Nothing could have induced him to undertake the ungrateful office of exposing these things, but the full persuasion that he was capable of convincing anything of an Englishman that had the least angle of his soul untainted with partiality, and that had the least concern left for the good of his country, that even the worst of these evils were easy to be cured; that if ever this nation were shipwrecked and undone, it must be at the very entrance of her port of deliverance, in the sight of her safety that Providence held out to her, in the sight of her safe establishment,

a prosperous trade, a regular, easily-supplied navy, and a
general reformation both in manners and methods in
Church and State.''

Defoe began as usual by laying down various clear
heads, under which he promised to deal with the whole
field of trade. But as usual he did not adhere to this
systematic plan. He discussed some topics of the day
with brilliant force, and then he suddenly digressed to
a subject only collaterally connected with trade. The
Queen, in opening the session of 1704-5, had exhorted her
Parliament to peace and union; but the High Churchmen were too hot to listen to advice even from her.
The Occasional Conformity Bill was again introduced
and carried in the Commons. The Lords rejected it.
The Commons persisted, and to secure the passing of
the measure, tacked it to a Bill of Supply. The
Lords refused to pass the Money Bill till the tack
was withdrawn. Soon afterwards the Parliament—Parliaments were then triennial—was dissolved, and the
canvass for a general election set in amidst unusual
excitement. Defoe abandoned the quiet topic of trade,
and devoted the *Review* to electioneering articles.

But he did not take a side, at least not a party side.
He took the side of peace and his country. "I saw
with concern," he said, in afterwards explaining his
position, "the weighty juncture of a new election for
members approach, the variety of wheels and engines
set to work in the nation, and the furious methods to
form interests on either hand and put the tempers of
men on all sides into an unusual motion; and things
seemed acted with so much animosity and party fury
that I confess it gave me terrible apprehensions of the
consequences." On both sides "the methods seemed to

him very scandalous." "In many places most horrid and villainous practices were set on foot to supplant one another. The parties stooped to vile and unbecoming meannesses; infinite briberies, forgeries, perjuries, and all manner of debauchings of the principles and manners of the electors were attempted. All sorts of violences, tumults, riots, breaches of the peace, neighbourhood, and good manners were made use of to support interests and carry elections." In short, Defoe saw the nation "running directly on the steep precipice of confusion." In these circumstances, he seriously reflected what he should do. He came to the conclusion that he must "immediately set himself in the *Review* to exhort, persuade, entreat, and in the most moving terms he was capable of prevail on all people in general to STUDY PEACE."

Under cover of this profession of impartiality, Defoe issued most effective attacks upon the High Church party. In order to promote peace, he said, it was necessary to ascertain first of all who were the enemies of peace. On the surface, the questions at stake in the elections were the privileges of the Dissenters and the respective rights of the Lords and the Commons in the matter of Money Bills. But people must look beneath the surface. "King James, French power, and a general turn of affairs was at the bottom, and the quarrels between Church and Dissenters only a politic noose they had hooked the parties on both sides into." Defoe lashed the Tackers into fury by his exhortations to the study of peace. He professed the utmost good-will to them personally, though he had not words strong enough to condemn their conduct in tacking the Occasional Bill to a Money Bill when they knew that the

F

Lords would reject it, and so in a moment of grave national peril leave the army without supplies. The Queen, in dissolving Parliament, had described this tacking as a dangerous experiment, and Defoe explained the experiment as being "whether losing the Money Bill, breaking up the Houses, disbanding the Confederacy, and opening the door to the French, might not have been for the interest of the High Church." Far be it from him to use Billingsgate language to the Tackers, but "the effect of their action, which, and not their motive, he had to consider, would undoubtedly be to let in the French, depose the Queen, bring in the Prince of Wales, abdicate the Protestant religion, restore Popery, repeal the Toleration, and persecute the Dissenters." Still it was probable that the Tackers meant no harm. *Humanum est errare.* He was certain that if he showed them their error, they would repent and be converted. All the same, he could not recommend them to the electors. "A Tacker is a man of passion, a man of heat, a man that is for ruining the nation upon any hazards to obtain his ends. Gentlemen freeholders, you must not choose a Tacker, unless you will destroy our peace, divide our strength, pull down the Church, let in the French, and depose the Queen."

From the dissolution of Parliament in April till the end of the year Defoe preached from this text with infinite variety and vigour. It is the chief subject of the second volume of the *Review.* The elections, powerfully influenced by Marlborough's successes as well as by the eloquent championship of Defoe, resulted in the entire defeat of the High Tories, and a further weeding of them out of high places in the Administration. Defoe was able to close this volume of the *Review* with expressions of delight at the attainment of the peace for which he had laboured, and, the victory being gained and the battle over, to promise a return to the intermitted subject of Trade. He returned to this subject in the beginning of his third volume. But he had not pursued it long when he was again called away. The second diversion, as he pointed out, was strictly analogous to the first. It was a summons to him to do his utmost to promote the union of the two kingdoms of England and Scotland. "From the same zeal," Defoe said, "with which I first pursued this blessed subject of peace, I found myself embarked in the further extent of it, I mean the Union. If I thought myself obliged in duty to the public interest to use my utmost endeavour to quiet the minds of enraged parties, I found myself under a stronger necessity to embark in the same design between two most enraged nations."

The union of the two kingdoms had become an object of pressing and paramount importance towards the close of William's reign. He had found little difficulty in getting the English Parliament to agree to settle the succession of the House of Hanover, but the proposal that the succession to the throne of Scotland should be settled on the same head was coldly received by the Scottish Parliament. It was not so much that the politicians of Edinburgh were averse to a common settlement, or positively eager for a King and Court of their own, but they were resolved to hold back till they were assured of commercial privileges which would go to compensate them for the drain of wealth that was supposed to have followed the King southwards. This was the policy of the wiser heads, not to accept the Union without as advantageous terms as they could secure. They had lost an opportunity at the Revolution, and were determined not to lose another. But among the mass of the population the feeling was all in favour of a separate kingdom. National animosity had been inflamed to a passionate pitch by the Darien disaster and the Massacre of Glencoe. The people listened readily to the insinuations of hot-headed men that the English wished to have everything their own way. The counter-charge about the Scotch found equally willing hearers among the mass in England. Never had cool-headed statesmen a harder task in preventing two nations from coming to blows. All the time that the Treaty of Union was being negotiated which King William had earnestly urged from his deathbed, throughout the first half of Queen Anne's reign they worked under a continual apprehension lest the negotiations should end in a violent and irreconcilable rupture.

Defoe might well say that he was pursuing the same blessed subject of Peace in trying to reconcile these two most enraged nations, and writing with all his might for the Union. An Act enabling the Queen to appoint Commissioners on the English side to arrange the terms of the Treaty had been passed in the first year of her reign but difficulties had arisen about the appointment of the Scottish Commissioners, and it was not till the Spring of 1706 that the two Commissions came together. When they did at last meet, they found each other much more reasonable and practical in spirit than had appeared possible during the battle over the preliminaries. But while the statesmen sat concocting the terms of the Treaty most amicably, from April to July, the excitement raged fiercely out of doors. Amidst the blaze of recriminations and counter-recriminations, Defoe moved energetically as the Apostle of Peace, making his *Review* play like a fireman's hose upon the flames. He did not try to persuade the Scotch to peace by the same methods which he had used in the case of the Highfliers and Tackers. His Reviews on this subject, full of spirit as ever, are models of the art of conciliation. He wrestled ardently with national prejudices on both sides, vindicating the Scotch Presbyterians from the charge of religious intolerance, labouring to prove that the English were not at all to blame for the collapse of the Darien expedition and the Glencoe tragedy, expounding what was fair to both nations in matters concerning trade. Abuse was heaped upon him plentifully by hot partisans; he was charged with want of patriotism from the one side, and with too much of it from the other; but he held on his way manfully, allowing no blow from his aspersers to pass unreturned. Seldom has so bold and skilful a soldier been enlisted in the cause of peace.

Defoe was not content with the *Review* as a literary instrument of pacification. He carried on the war in both capitals, answering the pamphlets of the Scotch patriots with counter-pamphlets from the Edinburgh press. He published also a poem, "in honour of Scotland," entitled *Caledonia*, with an artfully flattering preface, in which he declared the poem to be a simple tribute to the greatness of the people and the country without any reference whatever to the Union. Presently he found it expedient to make Edinburgh his headquarters, though he continued sending the *Review* three times a week to his London printer. When the Treaty of Union had been elaborated by the Commissioners and had passed the English Parliament, its difficulties

were not at an end. It had still to pass the Scotch
Parliament, and a strong faction there, riding on the
storm of popular excitement, insisted on discussing it
clause by clause. Moved partly by curiosity, partly by
earnest desire for the public good, according to his own
account in the *Review* and in his *History of the Union*,
Defoe resolved to undertake the "long, tedious, and
hazardous journey" to Edinburgh, and use all his influence to push the Treaty through. It was a task of no
small danger, for the prejudice against the Union went
so high in the Scottish capital that he ran the risk of
being torn to pieces by the populace. In one riot of
which he gives an account, his lodging was beset, and
for a time he was in as much peril "as a grenadier on a
counter-scarp." Still he went on writing pamphlets,
and lobbying members of Parliament. Owing to his
intimate knowledge of all matters relating to trade, he
also "had the honour to be frequently sent for into the
several Committees of Parliament which were appointed
to state some difficult points relating to equalities,
taxes, prohibitions, &c." Even when the Union was
agreed to by the Parliaments of both kingdoms, and took
effect formally in May 1707, difficulties arose in putting
the details in operation, and Defoe prolonged his stay
in Scotland through the whole of that year.

In this visit to Scotland Defoe protested to the world
at the time that he had gone as a diplomatist on his
own account, purely in the interests of peace. But a
suspicion arose and was very freely expressed, that both
in this journey and in previous journeys to the West and
the North of England during the elections, he was
serving as the agent, if not as the spy, of the Government. These reproaches he denied with indignation,

declaring it particularly hard that he should be subjected to such despiteful and injurious treatment even by writers "embarked in the same cause, and pretending to write for the same public good." "I contemn," he said in his *History*, "as not worth mentioning, the suggestions of some people, of my being employed thither to carry on the interest of a party. I have never loved any parties, but with my utmost zeal have sincerely espoused the great and original interest of this nation, and of all nations—I mean truth and liberty,— and whoever are of that party, I desire to be with them." He took up the same charges more passionately in the Preface to the third volume of the *Review*, and dealt with them in some brilliant passages of apologetic eloquence.

"I must confess," he said, "I have sometimes thought it very hard, that having voluntarily, without the least direction, assistance, or encouragement, in spite of all that has been suggested, taken upon me the most necessary work of removing national prejudices against the two most capital blessings of the world, Peace and Union, I should have the disaster to have the nations receive the doctrine and damn the teacher.

"Should I descend to particulars, it would hardly appear credible that in a Christian, a Protestant, and a Reformed nation, any man should receive such treatment as I have done, even from those very people whose consciences and judgments have stooped to the venerable truth, owned it has been useful, serviceable, and seasonable. . . .

"I am charged with partiality, bribery, pensions, and payments—a thing the circumstances, family, and fortunes of a man devoted to his country's peace clears me of. If paid, gentlemen, for writing, if hired, if employed, why still harassed with merciless and malicious men, why pursued to all extremities by law for old accounts, which you clear other men of every day ? Why oppressed, distressed, and driven from his family and from all his prospects of delivering them or himself ? Is this the fate of men employed and hired ? Is this the figure the agents of Courts and Princes make ? Certainly had I been hired or employed, those people who own the service would by this time have set their servant free from the little and implacable malice of litigious persecutions, murthering warrants, and men whose mouths are to be stopt by trifles. Let this suffice to clear me of all the little and scandalous charges of being hired and employed."

But then, people ask, if he was not officially employed, what had he to do with these affairs? Why should he meddle with them? To this he answers :—

"Truly, gentlemen, this is just the case. I saw a parcel of people caballing together to ruin property, corrupt the laws, invade the Government, debauch the people, and in short, enslave and embroil the nation, and I cried ' Fire !' or rather I cried ' Water !' for the fire was begun already. I see all the nation running into confusions and directly flying in the face of one another, and cried out ' Peace !' I called upon all sorts of people that had any senses to collect them together and judge for themselves what they were going to do, and excited them to lay hold of the madmen and take from them the wicked weapon, the knife with which they were going to destroy their mother, rip up the bowels of their country, and at last effectually ruin themselves.

" And what had I to do with this ? Why, yes, gentlemen, I had the same right as every man that has a footing in his country, or that has a posterity to possess liberty and claim right, must have, to preserve the laws, liberty, and government of that country to which he belongs, and he that charges me with meddling in what does not concern me, meddles himself with what 'tis plain he does not understand."

"I am not the first," Defoe said in another place, " that has been stoned for saying the truth. I cannot but think that as time and the conviction of their senses will restore men to love the peace now established in this nation, so they will gradually see I have acted no part but that of a lover of my country, and an honest man."

Time has undeniably shown that in these efforts to promote party peace and national union Defoe acted like a lover of his country, and that his aims were the aims of a statesmanlike as well as an honest man. And yet his protestations of independence and spontaneity of action, with all their ring of truth and all their solemnity of asseveration, were merely diplomatic blinds. He was all the time, as he afterwards admitted, when the admission could do no harm except to his own passing veracity, acting as the agent of Harley, and in enjoyment of an "appointment" from the Queen. What exactly the nature of his secret services in Scotland and elsewhere were, he very properly refused to reveal. His business probably was to ascertain and report the opinions of influential persons, and keep the Government informed as far as he could of the general state of feeling. At any rate it was not as he alleged, mere curiosity, or the fear of his creditors, or private enterprise, or pure and simple patriotic zeal that took Defoe to Scotland. The use he made of his debts as diplomatic instruments is curious. He not merely practised his faculties in the management of his creditors, which one of Lord Beaconsfield's characters commends as an incomparable means to a sound knowledge of human nature; but he made his debts actual pieces in his political game. His poverty, apparent, if not real, served as a screen for his employment under Government. When he was despatched on secret missions, he could depart wiping his eyes at the hardship of having to flee from his creditors.

CHAPTER VI.

DR. SACHEVERELL, AND THE CHANGE OF GOVERNMENT.

SOME of Defoe's biographers have claimed for him that he anticipated the doctrines of Free Trade. This is an error. It is true that Defoe was never tired of insisting, in pamphlets, books, and number after number of the *Review*, on the all-importance of trade to the nation. Trade was the foundation of England's greatness; success in trade was the most honourable patent of nobility; next to the maintenance of the Protestant religion, the encouragement of trade should be the chief care of English statesmen. On these heads Defoe's enthusiasm was boundless, and his eloquence inexhaustible. It is true also that he supported with all his might the commercial clauses of the Treaty of Utrecht, which sought to abolish the prohibitory duties on our trade with France. It is this last circumstance which has earned for him the repute of being a pioneer of Free-Trade. But his title to that repute does not bear examination. He was not so far in advance of his age as to detect the fallacy of the mercantile system. On the contrary, he avowed his adherence to it against those of his contemporaries who were inclined to call it in question. How Defoe came to support the new commercial treaty with France, and the grounds on which he supported it, can only be understood by looking at his relations with the Government.

While Defoe was living in Scotland in 1707, and filling the *Review* so exclusively with Scotch affairs that his readers, according to his own account, began to say that the fellow could talk of nothing but the Union, and had grown mighty dull of late, Harley's position in the Ministry was gradually becoming very insecure. He was suspected of cooling in his zeal for the war, and of keeping up clandestine relations with the Tories; and when Marlborough returned from his campaign at the close of the year he insisted upon the Secretary's dismissal. The Queen, who secretly resented the Marlborough yoke, at first refused her consent. Presently an incident occurred which gave them an excuse for more urgent pressure. One Gregg, a clerk in Harley's office, was discovered to be in secret correspondence with the French Court, furnishing Louis with the contents of important State papers. Harley was charged with complicity. This charge was groundless, but he could not acquit himself of gross negligence in the custody of his papers. Godolphin and Marlborough threatened to resign unless he was dismissed. Then the Queen yielded.

When Harley fell, Defoe, according to his own account in the *Appeal to Honour and Justice*, looked upon himself as lost, taking it for granted that "when a great officer fell, all who came in by his interest fall with him." But when his benefactor heard of this, and of Defoe's "resolution never to abandon the fortunes of the man to whom he owed so much," he kindly urged the devoted follower to think rather of his own interest than of any romantic obligation. "My lord Treasurer," he said, "will employ you in nothing but what is for the public service, and agreeably to your own sentiments of things; and besides, it is the Queen you are serving, who has been very good to you. Pray apply yourself as you used to do; I shall not take it ill from you in the least." To Godolphin accordingly Defoe applied himself, was by him introduced a second time to Her Majesty and to the honour of kissing her hand, and obtained "the continuance of an appointment which Her Majesty had been pleased to make him in consideration of a former special service he had done." This was the appointment which he held while he was challenging his enemies to say whether his outward circumstances looked like the figure the agents of Courts and Princes make.

The services on which Defoe was employed were, as before, of two kinds, active and literary. Shortly after the change in the Ministry early in 1708, news came of the gathering of the French expedition at Dunkirk, with a view, it was suspected, of trying to effect a landing in Scotland. Defoe was at once despatched to Edinburgh on an errand which, he says, was "far from being unfit for a sovereign to direct or an honest man to perform." If his duties were to mix with the people and ascertain the state of public feeling, and more specifically to sound suspected characters, to act, in short, as a political detective or spy, the service was one which it was essential that the Government should get some trustworthy person to undertake, and which any man at such a crisis might perform, if he could, without any discredit to his honesty or his patriotism. The independence of the sea-girt realm was never in greater peril. The French expedition was a well-conceived diversion, and it was imperative that the Government should know on what amount of support the invaders might rely in the bitterness prevailing in Scotland after the Union. Fortunately the loyalty of the Scotch Jacobites was not put to the test. As in the case of the Spanish Armada, accident fought on our side. The French fleet succeeded in reaching the coast of Scotland before the ships of the defenders; but it overshot its arranged landing-point, and had no hope but to sail back ingloriously to Dunkirk. Meantime, Defoe had satisfactorily discharged himself of his mission. Godolphin showed his appreciation of his services by recalling him as soon as Parliament was dissolved, to travel through the counties and serve the cause of the Government in the general elections. He was frequently sent to Scotland again on similarly secret errands, and seems to have established a printing business there, made arrangements for the simultaneous issue of the *Review* in Edinburgh and London, besides organizing Edinburgh newspapers, executing commissions for English merchants, and setting on foot a linen manufactory.

But we are more concerned with the literary labours of this versatile and indefatigable genius. These, in the midst of his multifarious commercial and diplomatic concerns, he never intermitted. All the time the *Review* continued to give a brilliant support to the Ministry. The French expedition had lent a new interest to the affairs of Scotland, and Defoe advertised, that though he never intended to make the *Review* a newspaper, circumstances enabled him to furnish exceptionally correct intelligence from Scotland as well as sound impartial opinions. The intelligence which he communicated was all with a purpose, and a good purpose—the promotion

of a better understanding between the united nations.
He never had a better opportunity for preaching from
his favourite text of Peace and Union, and he used it
characteristically, championing the cause of the Scotch
Presbyterians, asserting the firmness of their loyalty,
smoothing over trading grievances by showing elabo-
rately how both sides benefited from the arrangements
of the Union, launching shafts in every direction at his
favourite butts, and never missing a chance of exulting
in his own superior wisdom. In what a posture would
England have been now, he cried, if those wiseacres had
been listened to, who were for trusting the defence of
England solely to the militia and the fleet ! Would our
fleet have kept the French from landing if Providence
had not interposed ; and if they had landed, would a
militia, undermined by disaffection, have been able to
beat them back ? The French king deserved a vote of
thanks for opening the eyes of the nation against foolish
advisers, and for helping it to heal internal divisions.
Louis, poor gentleman, was much to be pitied, for his
informers had evidently served him badly, and had led
him to expect a greater amount of support from disloyal
factions than they had the will or the courage to give
him.

During the electoral canvass, Defoe surpassed himself
in the lively vigour of his advocacy of the Whig cause.
"And now, gentlemen of England," he began in the
Review—as it went on he became more and more direct
and familiar in his manner of addressing his readers—
"now we are a-going to choose Parliament men, I will
tell you a story." And he proceeded to tell how in a
certain borough a great patron procured the election of
a " shock dog " as its parliamentary representative.

Money and ale, Defoe says, could do anything. "God knows I speak it with regret for you all and for your posterity, it is not an impossible thing to debauch this nation into a choice of thieves, knaves, devils, shock dogs, or anything comparatively speaking, by the power of various intoxications." He spent several numbers of the *Review* in an ironical advice to the electors to choose Tories, showing with all his skill "the mighty and prevailing reason why we should have a Tory Parliament." "O gentlemen," he cried, "if we have any mind to buy some more experience, be sure and choose Tories." "We want a little instruction, we want to go to school to knaves and fools." Afterwards, dropping this thin mask, he declared that among the electors only "the drunken, the debauched, the swearing, the persecuting" would vote for the Highfliers. "The grave, the sober, the thinking, the prudent," would vote for the Whigs. "A House of Tories is a House of Devils." "If ever we have a Tory Parliament, the nation is undone." In his *Appeal to Honour and Justice* Defoe explained, that while he was serving Godolphin, "being resolved to remove all possible ground of suspicion that he kept any secret correspondence, he never visited, or wrote to, or any way corresponded with his principal benefactor for above three years." Seeing that Harley was at that time the leader of the party which Defoe was denouncing with such spirit, it would have been strange indeed if there had been much intercourse between them.

Though regarded after his fall from office as the natural leader of the Tory party, Harley was a very reserved politician, who kept his own counsel, used instruments of many shapes and sizes, steered clear of

entangling engagements, and left himself free to take
advantage of various opportunities. To wage war against
the Ministry was the work of more ardent partisans.
He stood by and waited while Bolingbroke and Rochester
and their allies in the press cried out that the Government was now in the hands of the enemies of the Church,
accused the Whigs of protracting the war to fill their
own pockets with the plunder of the Supplies, and called
upon the nation to put an end to their jobbery and mismanagement. The victory of Oudenarde in the summer
of 1708 gave them a new handle. " What is the good,"
they cried, " of these glorious victories, if they do not
bring peace ? What do we gain by beating the French
in campaign after campaign, if we never bring them
nearer to submission ? It is incredible that the French
King is not willing to make peace, if the Whigs did not
profit too much by the war to give peace any encourage_
ment." To these arguments for peace, Defoe opposed
himself steadily in the *Review*. " Well, gentlemen," he
began, when the news came of the battle of Oudenarde,
" have the French noosed themselves again ? Let us
pray the Duke of Marlborough that a speedy peace may
not follow, for what would become of us ? " He was as
willing for a peace on honourable terms as any man, but
a peace till the Protestant Succession was secured and
the balance of power firmly settled, " would be fatal to
peace at home." " If that fatal thing called Peace abroad
should happen, we shall certainly be undone." Presently,
however, the French king began to make promising
overtures for peace; the Ministry in hopes of satisfactory terms encouraged them; the talk through the
nation was all of peace, and the Whigs contented themselves with passing an address to the Crown through

Parliament urging the Queen to make no peace till the Pretender should be disowned by the French Court, and the Succession guaranteed by a compact with the Allies. Throughout the winter the *Review* expounded with brilliant clearness the only conditions on which an honourable peace could be founded, and prepared the nation to doubt the sincerity with which Louis had entered into negotiations. Much dissatisfaction was felt, and that dissatisfaction was eagerly fanned by the Tories when the negotiations fell through, in consequence of the distrust with which the allies regarded Louis, and their imposing upon him too hard a test of his honesty Defoe fought vigorously against the popular discontent. The charges against Marlborough were idle rhodomontade. We had no reason to be discouraged with the progress of the war unless we had formed extravagant expectations. Though the French king's resources had been enfeebled, and he might reasonably have been expected to desire peace, he did not care for the welfare of France so much as for his own glory; he would fight to gain his purpose while there was a pistole in his treasury, and we must not expect Paris to be taken in a week. Nothing could be more admirable than Godolphin's management of our own Treasury ; he deserved almost more credit than the Duke himself. " Your Treasurer has been your general of generals ; without his exquisite management of the cash the Duke of Marlborough must have been beaten."

The Sacheverell incident, which ultimately led to the overthrow of the Ministry, gave Defoe a delightful opening for writing in their defence. A collection of his articles on this subject would show his controversial style at its best and brightest. Sacheverell and he

G

were old antagonists. Sacheverell's "bloody flag and banner of defiance," and other Highflying truculencies, had furnished him with the main basis of his *Shortest Way with the Dissenters*. The laugh of the populace was then on Defoe's side, partly, perhaps, because the Government had prosecuted him. But in the changes of the troubled times, the Oxford Doctor, nurtured in "the scolding of the ancients," had found a more favourable opportunity. His literary skill was of the most mechanical kind, but at the close of 1709, when hopes of peace had been raised only to be disappointed, and the country was suffering from the distress of a prolonged war, people were more in a mood to listen to a preacher who disdained to check the sweep of his rhetoric by qualifications or abatements, and luxuriated in denouncing the Queen's Ministers from the pulpit under scriptural allegories. He delivered a tremendous philippic about the Perils of False Brethren, as a sermon before the Lord Mayor in November. It would have been a wise thing for the Ministry to have left Sacheverell to be dealt with by their supporters in the press and in the pulpit. But in an evil hour Godolphin, stung by a nickname thrown at him by the rhetorical priest—a singularly comfortable-looking man to have so virulent a tongue, one of those orators who thrive on ill-conditioned language—resolved, contrary to the advice of more judicious colleagues, to have him impeached by the House of Commons. The Commons readily voted the sermon seditious, scandalous, and malicious, and agreed to a resolution for his impeachment; the Lords ordered that the case should be heard at their bar; and Westminster Hall was prepared to be the scene of a great public trial. At first Defoe, in heaping contemptuous ridicule upon the Highflying Doctor, had spoken as if he would consider prosecution a blunder. The man ought rather to be encouraged to go on exposing himself and his party. "Let him go on," he said, "to bully Moderation, explode Toleration, and damn the Union; the gain will be ours."

"You should use him as we do a hot horse. When he first frets and pulls, keep a stiff rein and hold him in if you can; but if he grows mad and furious, slack your hand, clap your heels to him, and let him go. Give him his belly full of it. Away goes the beast like a fury over hedge and ditch, till he runs himself off his mettle; perhaps bogs himself, and then he grows quiet of course. . . . Besides, good people, do you not know the nature of the barking creatures? If you pass but by, and take no notice, they will yelp and make a noise, and perhaps run a little after you; but turn back, offer to strike them or throw stones at them, and you'll never have done—nay, you'll raise all the dogs of the parish upon you."

This last was precisely what the Government did, and they found reason to regret that they did not take Defoe's advice and let Sacheverell alone. When, however, they did resolve to prosecute him, Defoe immediately turned round, and exulted in the prosecution as the very thing which he had foreseen. "Was not the *Review* right when he said you ought to let such people run on till they were out of breath? Did I not note to you that precipitations have always ruined them and served us? . . . . Not a hound in the pack opened like him. He has done the work effectually. . . . He has raised the house and waked the landlady. . . . Thank him, good people, thank him and clap him on the back; let all his party do but this, and the day is our own." Nor did

Defoe omit to remind the good people that he had been
put in the pillory for satirically hinting that the High
Church favoured such doctrines as Sacheverell was now
prosecuted for. In his *Hymn to the Pillory* he had
declared that Sacheverell ought to stand there in his
place. His wish was now gratified; "the bar of the
House of Commons is the worst pillory in the nation."
In the two months which elapsed before the trial,
during which the excitement was steadily growing,
Sacheverell and his doctrines were the main topic of the
Review. If a popular tempest could have been allayed
by brilliant argument, Defoe's papers ought to have
done it. He was a manly antagonist, and did not
imitate coarser pamphleteers in raking up scandals
about the Doctor's private life—at least not under his
own name. There was, indeed, a pamphlet issued by
"a Gentleman of Oxford," which bears many marks of
Defoe's authorship, and contains an account of some
passages in Sacheverell's life not at all to the clergy-
man's credit. But the only pamphlet outside the *Review*
which the biographers have ascribed to Defoe's activity,
is a humorous Letter from the Pope to Don Sacheverellio,
giving him· instructions how to advance the interest of
the Pretender. In the *Review* Defoe, treating Sacheverell with riotously mirthful contempt, calls for the
punishment of the doctrines rather than the man. During
the trial, which lasted more than a fortnight, a mob
attended the Doctor's carriage every day from his lodgings
in the Temple to Westminster Hall, huzzaing, and pressing to kiss his hand, and spent the evenings in rabbling
the Dissenters' meeting-houses, and hooting before the
residences of prominent Whigs. Defoe had always said
that the Highfliers would use violence to their opponents

if they had the power, and here was a confirmation of his opinion on which he did not fail to insist. The sentence on Sacheverell, that his sermon and vindication should be burnt by the common hangman and himself suspended from preaching for three years, was hailed by the mob as an acquittal, and celebrated by tumultuous gatherings and bonfires. Defoe reasoned hard and joyfully to prove that the penalty was everything that could be wished, and exactly what he had all along advised and contemplated, but he did not succeed in persuading the masses that the Government had not suffered a defeat.

The impeachment of Sacheverell turned popular feeling violently against the Whigs. The break up of the Gertruydenberg Conference without peace gave a strong push in the same direction. It was all due, the Tories shouted, and the people were now willing to believe, to the folly of our Government in insisting upon impossible conditions from the French king, and their shameless want of patriotism in consulting the interests of the Allies rather than of England. The Queen, who for some time had been longing to get rid of her Whig Ministers, did not at once set sail with this breeze. She dismissed the Earl of Sunderland in June, and sent word to her allies that she meant to make no further changes. Their ambassadors, with what was even then resented as an impertinence, congratulated her on this resolution, and then in August she took the momentous step of dismissing Godolphin, and putting the Treasury nominally in commission, but really under the management of Harley. For a few weeks it seems to have been Harley's wish to conduct the administration in concert with the remaining Whig members, but the extreme

Tories, with whom he had been acting, overbore his
moderate intentions.   They threatened to desert him
unless he broke clearly and definitely with the Whigs.
In October accordingly the Whigs were all turned out
of the Administration, Tories put in their places, Parliament dissolved, and writs issued for new elections.
"So sudden and entire a change of the Ministry,"
Bishop Burnet remarks, "is scarce to be found in our
history, especially where men of great abilities had
served both with zeal and success." That the Queen
should dismiss one or all of her Ministers in the face of
a Parliamentary majority excited no surprise; but that
the whole Administration should be changed at a stroke
from one party to the other was a new and strange thing.
The old Earl of Sunderland's suggestion to William III.
had not taken root in constitutional practice; this was
the fulfilment of it under the gradual pressure of
circumstances.

Defoe's conduct while the political balance was rock-
ing, and after the Whig side had decisively kicked the
beam, is a curious study.   One hardly knows which to
admire most, the loyalty with which he stuck to the
falling house till the moment of its collapse, or the
adroitness with which he escaped from the ruins.   Cen-
sure of his shiftiness is partly disarmed by the fact that
there were so many in that troubled and uncertain time
who would have acted like him if they had had the skill.
Besides, he acted so steadily and with such sleepless
vigilance and energy on the principle that the appearance of honesty is the best policy, that at this distance
of time it is not easy to catch him tripping, and if we
refuse to be guided by the opinion of his contemporaries,
we almost inevitably fall victims to his incomparable

plausibility. Deviations in his political writings from the course of the honest patriot are almost as difficult to detect as flaws in the verisimilitude of *Robinson Crusoe* or the *Journal of the Plague.*

During the two months' interval between the substitution of Dartmouth for Sunderland and the fall of Godolphin, Defoe used all his powers of eloquence and argument to avert the threatened changes in the Ministry, and keep the Tories out. He had a personal motive for this, he confessed. "My own share in the ravages they shall make upon our liberties is like to be as severe as any man's, from the rage and fury of a party who are in themselves implacable, and whom God has not been pleased to bless me with a talent to flatter and submit to." Of the dismissed minister Sunderland, with whom Defoe had been in personal relations during the negotiations for the Union, he spoke in terms of the warmest praise, always with a formal profession of not challenging the Queen's judgment in discharging her servant. "My Lord Sunderland," he said, "leaves the Ministry with the most unblemished character that ever I read of any statesman in the world." "I am making no court to my Lord Sunderland. The unpolished author of this paper never had the talent of making his court to the great men of the age." But where is the objection against his conduct? Not a dog of the party can bark against him. "They cannot show me a man of their party that ever did act like him, or of whom they can say we should believe he would if he had the opportunity." The Tories were clamouring for the dismissal of all the other Whigs. High Church addresses to the Queen were pouring in, claiming to represent the sense of the nation, and hinting an absolute want of

confidence in the Administration. Defoe examined the
conduct of the Ministers severally and collectively, and
demanded where was the charge against them, where
the complaint, where the treasure misapplied?

As for the sense of the nation, there was one sure
way of testing this better than any got-up addresses,
namely, the rise or fall of the public credit. The public
stocks fell immediately on the news of Sunderland's
dismissal, and were only partially revived upon Her
Majesty's assurance to the Directors of the Bank that
she meant to keep the Ministry otherwise unchanged.
A rumour that Parliament was to be dissolved had sent
them down again. If the public credit is thus affected
by the mere apprehension of a turn of affairs in
England, Defoe said, the thing itself will be a fatal
blow to it. The coy Lady Credit had been wavering
in her attachment to England; any sudden change
would fright her away altogether. As for the pooh-pooh
cry of the Tories that the national credit was of no consequence, that a nation could not be in debt to itself,
and that their moneyed men would come forward with
nineteen shillings in the pound for the support of the
war, Defoe treated this claptrap with proper ridicule.

But in spite of all Defoe's efforts, the crash came.
On the 10th of August the Queen sent to Godolphin for
the Treasurer's staff, and Harley became her Prime
Minister. How did Defoe behave then? The first two
numbers of the *Review* after the Lord Treasurer's fall
are among the most masterly of his writings. He was
not a small, mean, timid time-server and turncoat. He
faced about with bold and steady caution, on the alert
to give the lie to anybody who dared to accuse him of
facing about at all. He frankly admitted that he was

in a quandary what to say about the change that had taken place. "If a man could be found that could sail north and south, that could speak truth and falsehood, that could turn to the right hand and the left, all at the same time, he would be the man, he would be the only proper person that should now speak." Of one thing only he was certain. "We are sure honest men go out." As for their successors, "it is our business to hope, and time must answer for those that come in. If Tories, if Jacobites, if Highfliers, if madmen of any kind are to come in, I am against them; I ask them no favour, I make no court to them, nor am I going about to please them." But the question was, what was to be done in the circumstances? Defoe stated plainly two courses, with their respective dangers. To cry out about the new Ministry was to ruin public credit. To profess cheerfulness was to encourage the change and strengthen the hands of those that desired to push it farther. On the whole, for himself he considered the first danger the most to be dreaded of the two. Therefore he announced his intention of devoting his whole energy to maintaining the public credit, and advised all true Whigs to do likewise. "Though I don't like the crew, I won't sink the ship. I'll do my best to save the ship. I'll pump and heave and haul, and do anything I can, though he that pulls with me were my enemy. The reason is plain. We are all in the ship, and must sink or swim together."

What could be more plausible? What conduct more truly patriotic? Indeed, it would be difficult to find fault with Defoe's behaviour, were it not for the rogue's protestations of inability to court the favour of great men, and his own subsequent confessions in his *Appeal*

to Honour and Justice, as to what took place behind the
scenes.   Immediately on the turn of affairs he took
steps to secure that connexion with the Government, the
existence of which he was always denying.   The day
after Godolphin's displacement, he tells us, he waited
on him, and "humbly asked his lordship's direction what
course he should take."   Godolphin at once assured him,
in very much the same words that Harley had used
before, that the change need make no difference to him ;
he was the Queen's servant, and all that had been done
for him was by Her Majesty's special and particular
direction ; his business was to wait till he saw things
settled, and then apply himself to the Ministers of
State, to receive Her Majesty's commands from them.
Thereupon Defoe resolved to guide himself by the
following principle :—

   "It occurred to me immediately, as a principle for my conduct, that it was not material to me what ministers Her
Majesty was pleased to employ ; my duty was to go along
with every Ministry, so far as they did not break in upon
the Constitution, and the laws and liberties of my country ;
my part being only the duty of a subject, viz. to submit to
all lawful commands, and to enter into no service which was
not justifiable by the laws ; to all which I have exactly
obliged myself."

   Defoe was thus, as he says, providentially cast back
upon his original benefactor.   That he received any
consideration, pension, gratification, or reward for his
services to Harley, "except that old appointment which
Her Majesty was pleased to make him," he strenuously
denied.   The denial is possibly true, and it is extremely
probable that he was within the truth when he protested in the most solemn manner that he had never

"received any instructions, directions, orders, or let
them call it what they will, of that kind, for the
writing of any part of what he had written, or any
materials for the putting together, for the forming any
book or pamphlet whatsoever, from the said Earl of
Oxford, late Lord Treasurer, or from any person by his
order or direction, since the time that the late Earl of
Godolphin was Lord Treasurer." Defoe declared that
"in all his writing, he ever capitulated for his liberty
to speak according to his own judgment of things," and
we may easily believe him. He was much too clever a
servant to need instructions.

His secret services to Harley in the new elections are
probably buried in oblivion. In the *Review* he pursued
a strain which to the reader who does not take his
articles in connexion with the politics of the time,
might appear to be thoroughly consistent with his
advice to the electors on previous occasions. He meant
to confine himself, he said at starting, rather to the
manner of choosing than to the persons to be chosen,
and he never denounced bribery, intimidation, rioting,
rabbling, and every form of interference with the
electors' freedom of choice, in more energetic language.
As regarded the persons to be chosen, his advice was as
before, to choose moderate men—men of sense and
temper, not men of fire and fury. But he no longer
asserted, as he had done before, the exclusive possession
of good qualities by the Whigs. He now recognised
that there were hot Whigs as well as moderate Whigs,
moderate Tories as well as hot Tories. It was for the
nation to avoid both extremes and rally round the men
of moderation, whether Whig or Tory. " If we have a
Tory Highflying Parliament, we Tories are undone.

If we have a hot Whig Parliament, we Whigs are undone."

The terms of Defoe's advice were unexceptionable, but the Whigs perceived a change from the time when he declared that if ever we have a Tory Parliament, the nation is undone. It was as if a Republican writer after the *coup d'état* of the 16th May, 1877, had warned the French against electing extreme Republicans, and had echoed the Marshal-President's advice to give their votes to moderate men of all parties. Defoe did not increase the conviction of his party loyalty when a Tory Parliament was returned, by trying to prove that whatever the new members might call themselves they must inevitably be Whigs. He admitted in the most unqualified way that the elections had been disgracefully riotous and disorderly, and lectured the constituencies freely on their conduct. " It is not," he said, " a Free Parliament that you have chosen. You have met, mobbed, rabbled, and thrown dirt at one another, but election by mob is no more free election than Oliver's election by a standing army. Parliaments and rabbles are contrary things." Yet he had hopes of the gentlemen who had been thus chosen.

" I have it upon many good grounds, as I think I told you, that there are some people who are shortly to come together, of whose character, let the people that send them up think what they will, when they come thither, they will not run the mad length that is expected of them ; they will act upon the Revolution principle, keep within the circle of the law, proceed with temper, moderation, and justice, to support the same interest we have all carried on—and this I call being Whiggish, or acting as Whigs.

" I shall not trouble you with further examining why they will be so, or why they will act thus ; I think it is so plain from the necessity of the Constitution and the circumstances of things before them, that it needs no further demonstration —they will be Whigs, they must be Whigs ; there is no remedy, for the Constitution is a Whig."

The new members of Parliament must either be Whigs or traitors, for everybody who favours the Protestant succession is a Whig, and everybody who does not is a traitor.   Defoe used the same ingenuity in playing upon words in his arguments in support of the public credit.   Every true Whig, he argued, in the *Review* and in separate essays, was bound to uphold the public credit, for to permit it to be impaired was the surest way to let in the Pretender.   The Whigs were accused of withdrawing their money from the public stocks, to mark their distrust of the Government.   "Nonsense," Defoe said, "in that case they would not be Whigs."   Naturally enough, as the *Review* now practically supported a Ministry in which extreme Tories had the predominance, he was upbraided for having gone over to that party.   "Why, gentlemen," he retorted, "it would be more natural for you to think I am turned Turk than High-flier; and to make me a Mahometan would not be half so ridiculous as to make me say the Whigs are running down credit, when on the contrary I am still satisfied if there were no Whigs at this time, there would hardly be any such thing as credit left among us."   "If the credit of the nation is to be maintained, we must all act as Whigs, because credit can be maintained upon no other foot.   Had the doctrine of non-resistance of tyranny been voted, had the Prerogative been exalted above the Law, and property subjected to absolute will, would Parliament have voted the funds?   Credit supposes Whigs lending and a Whig Government borrowing. It is nonsense to talk of credit and passive submission."

Had Defoe confined himself to lecturing those hot Whigs who were so afraid of the secret Jacobitism of Harley's colleagues that they were tempted to withdraw their money from the public stocks, posterity, unable to judge how far these fears were justified, and how far it was due to a happy accident that they were not realized, might have given him credit for sacrificing partisanship to patriotism. This plea could hardly be used for another matter in which, with every show of reasonable fairness, he gave a virtual support to the Ministry. We have seen how he spoke of Marlborough, and Godolphin's management of the army and the finances when the Whigs were in office. When the Tories came in, they at once set about redeeming their pledges to inquire into the malversation of their predecessors. Concerning this proceeding, Defoe spoke with an approval which, though necessarily guarded in view of his former professions of extreme satisfaction, was none the less calculated to recommend.

"Inquiry into miscarriages in things so famous and so fatal as war and battle is a thing so popular that no man can argue against it ; and had we paid well, and hanged well, much sooner, as some men had not been less in a condition to mistake, so some others might not have been here to find fault. But it is better late than never ; when the inquiry is set about heartily, it may be useful on several accounts, both to unravel past errors and to prevent new. For my part, as we have for many years past groaned for want of justice upon wilful mistakes, yet, in hopes some of the careful and mischievous designing gentlemen may come in for a share, I am glad the work is begun."

With equal good humour and skill in leaving open
a double interpretation, he commented on the fact that
the new Parliament did not, as had been customary, give
a formal vote of thanks to Marlborough for his conduct
of his last campaign.

" We have had a mighty pother here in print about reward-
ing of generals.   Some think great men too much rewarded,
and some think them too little rewarded.   The case is so nice,
neither side will bear me to speak my mind ; but I am persuaded of this, that there is no general has or ever will
merit great things of us, but he has received and will receive
all the grateful acknowledgments he OUGHT to expect."

But his readers would complain that he had not de-
fined the word " ought."   That, he said, with audacious
pleasantry, he left to them.   And while they were on
the subject of mismanagement, he would give them a
word of advice which he had often given them before.
" While you bite and devour one another, you are all
mismanagers.   Put an end to your factions, your
tumults, your rabbles, or you will not be able to make
war upon anybody."   Previously, however, his way of
making peace at home was to denounce the High-fliers.
He was still pursuing the same object, though by a
different course, now that the leaders of the High-fliers
were in office, when he declared that "those Whigs who
say that the new Ministry is entirely composed of Tories
and High-fliers are fool-Whigs."   The remark was no
doubt perfectly true, but yet if Defoe had been thoroughly
consistent he ought at least, instead of supporting the
Ministry on account of the small moderate element it
contained, to have urged its purification from dangerous
ingredients.

This, however, it must be admitted, he also did, though
indirectly and at a somewhat later stage, when Harley's
tenure of the Premiership was menaced by Highfliers
who thought him much too lukewarm a leader. A
" cave," the famous October Club, was formed in the
autumn of 1711, to urge more extreme measures upon
the ministry against Whig officials, and to organize a
High Church agitation throughout the country. It consisted chiefly of country squires, who wished to see
members of the late Ministry impeached, and the Duke
of Marlborough dismissed from the command of the
army. At Harley's instigation Swift wrote an " advice "
to these hot partisans, beseeching them to have patience
and trust the Ministry, and everything that they wished
would happen in due time. Defoe sought to break their
ranks by a direct onslaught in his most vigorous style,
denouncing them in the *Review* as Jacobites in disguise
and an illicit importation from France, and writing
their " secret history," " with some friendly characters
of the illustrious members of that honourable society "
in two separate tracts. This skirmish served the double
purpose of strengthening Harley against the reckless
zealots of his party, and keeping up Defoe's appearance
of impartiality. Throughout the fierce struggle of
parties, never so intense in any period of our history as
during those years when the Constitution itself hung in
the balance, it was as a True-born Englishman first and
a Whig and Dissenter afterwards, that Defoe gave his
support to the Tory Ministry. It may not have been
his fault ; he may have been most unjustly suspected ;
but nobody at the time would believe his protestations of
independence. When his former High-flying persecutor,
the Earl of Nottingham, went over to the Whigs and

with their acquiescence, or at least without their active opposition, introduced another Bill to put down Occasional Conformity, Defoe wrote trenchantly against it. But even then the Dissenters, as he loudly lamented, repudiated his alliance. The Whigs were not so much pleased on this occasion with his denunciations of the persecuting spirit of the High Churchmen, as they were enraged by his stinging taunts levelled at themselves for abandoning the Dissenters to their persecutors. The Dissenters must now see, Defoe said, that they would not be any better off under a Low Church ministry than under a High Church ministry. But the Dissenters, considering that the Whigs were too much in a minority to prevent the passing of the Bill, however willing to do so, would only see in their professed champion an artful supporter of the men in power.

A curious instance has been preserved of the estimate of Defoe's character at this time.[1] M. Mesnager, an agent sent by the French King to sound the Ministry and the country as to terms of peace, wanted an able pamphleteer to promote the French interest. The Swedish Resident recommended Defoe, who had just issued a tract entitled, *Reasons why this Nation ought to put an end to this expensive War.* Mesnager was delighted with the tract, at once had it translated into French and circulated through the Netherlands, employed the Swede to treat with Defoe, and sent him a hundred pistoles by way of earnest. Defoe kept the pistoles, but told the Queen, M. Mesnager recording that though " he missed his aim in this person, the money perhaps was not

---

[1] I doubt whether it adds to the credibility of the story in all points that the minutes of M. Mesnager's Negotiations were "translated," and probably composed by Defoe himself. See p. 139.

wholly lost; for I afterwards understood that the man
was in the service of the state, and that he had let the
Queen know of the hundred pistoles he had received;
so I was obliged to sit still, and be very well satisfied
that I had not discovered myself to him, for it was not
our season yet." The anecdote at once shows the
general opinion entertained of Defoe, and the fact that
he was less corruptible than was supposed. There can
be little doubt that our astute intriguer would have
outwitted the French emissary if he had not been
warned in time, pocketed his bribes, and wormed
his secrets out of him for the information of the
Government.

During Godolphin's Ministry, Defoe's cue had been
to reason with the nation against too impatient a
longing for peace. Let us have peace by all means,
had been his text, but not till honourable terms have
been secured, and meantime the war is going on as
prosperously as any but madmen can desire. He re-
peatedly challenged adversaries who compared what
he wrote then with what he wrote under the new
Ministry, to prove him guilty of inconsistency. He
stood on safe ground when he made this challenge,
for circumstances had changed sufficiently to justify
any change of opinion. The plans of the Confederates
were disarranged by the death of the Emperor, and
the accession of his brother, the Archduke Charles,
to the vacant crown. To give the crown of Spain in
these new circumstances to the Archduke, as had been
the object of the Allies when they began the war,
would have been as dangerous to the balance of power
as to let Spain pass to Louis's grandson, Philip of
Anjou. It would be more dangerous, Defoe argued;

and by far the safest course would be to give Spain to Philip and his posterity, who "would be as much Spaniards in a very short time, as ever Philip II. was or any of his other predecessors." This was the main argument which had been used in the latter days of King William against going to war at all, and Defoe had then refuted it scornfully ; but circumstances had changed, and he not only adopted it, but also issued an essay "proving that it was always the sense both of King William and of all the Confederates, and even of the Grand Alliance itself, that the Spanish monarchy should never be united in the person of the Emperor." Partition the Spanish dominions in Europe between France and Germany, and the West Indies between England and Holland—such was Defoe's idea of a proper basis of peace.

But while Defoe expounded in various forms the conditions of a good peace, he devoted his main energy to proving that peace under some conditions was a necessity. He dilated on the enormous expense of the war, and showed by convincing examples that it was ruining the trade of the country. Much that he said was perfectly true, but if he had taken M. Mesnager's bribes and loyally carried out his instructions, he could not more effectually have served the French King's interests than by writing as he did at that juncture. The proclaimed necessity under which England lay to make peace, offered Louis an advantage which he was not slow to take. The proposals which he made at the Congress of Utrecht, and which he had ascertained would be accepted by the English Ministry and the Queen, were not unjustly characterised by the indignant Whigs as being such as he might have made

H 2

at the close of a successful war. The territorial con-
cessions to England and Holland were insignificant;
the States were to have the right of garrisoning certain
barrier-towns in Flanders, and England was to have
some portions of Canada. But there was no mention
of dividing the West Indies between them—the West
Indies were to remain attached to Spain. It was the
restoration of their trade that was their main desire in
these great commercial countries, and even that object
Louis agreed to promote in a manner that seemed,
according to the ideas of the time, to be more to his
own advantage than to theirs. In the case of England,
he was to remove prohibitions against our imports, and
in return we engaged to give the French imports the
privileges of the most favoured nations. In short,
we were to have free trade with France, which the
commercial classes of the time looked upon as a very
doubtful blessing.

It is because Defoe wrote in favour of this free trade
that he is supposed to have been superior to the commercial fallacies of the time. But a glance at his arguments shows that this is a very hasty inference. It was no
part of Defoe's art as a controversialist to seek to correct
popular prejudices; on the contrary, it was his habit to
take them for granted as the bases of his arguments, to
work from them as premises towards his conclusion.
He expressly avowed himself a prohibitionist in principle :—

"I am far from being of their mind who say that all prohibitions are destructive to trade, and that wise nations, the
Dutch, make no prohibitions at all.

"Where any nation has, by the singular blessing of
God, a produce given to their country from which such a

manufacture can be made as other nations cannot be without, and none can make that produce but themselves, it would be distraction in that nation not to prohibit the exportation of that original produce till it is manufactured."

He had been taunted with flying in the face of what he had himself said in King William's time in favour of prohibition. But he boldly undertakes to prove that prohibition was absolutely necessary in King William's time, and not only so, but that "the advantages we may make of taking off a prohibition now, are all founded upon the advantages we did make of laying on a prohibition then; that the same reason which made a prohibition then the best thing, makes it now the maddest thing a nation could do or ever did in the matter of trade." In King William's time, the balance of trade was against us to the extent of 850,000l., in consequence of the French King's laying extravagant duties upon the import of all our woollen manufactures.

"Whoever thinks that by opening the French trade I should mean . . . that we should come to trade with them 850,000l. *per annum* to our loss, must think me as mad as I think him for suggesting it; but if, on the contrary, I prove that as we traded then 850,000l. a year to our loss, we can trade now with them 600,000l. to our gain, then I will venture to draw this consequence, that we are distracted, speaking of our trading wits, if we do not trade with them."

In a preface to the Eighth Volume of the *Review* (July 29, 1712), Defoe announced his intention of discontinuing the publication, in consequence of the tax then imposed on newspapers. We can hardly suppose that this was his real motive, and as a matter of fact the *Review*, whose death had been announced, reappeared in due course in the form of a single leaf, and was published in that form till the 11th of June, 1713. By that time a new project was on foot which Defoe had frequently declared his intention of starting, a paper devoted exclusively to the discussion of the affairs of trade. The *Review* at one time had declared its main subject to be trade, but had claimed a liberty of digression under which the main subject had all but disappeared. At last, however, in May, 1713, when popular excitement and hot Parliamentary debates were expected on the Commercial Treaty with France, an exclusively trading paper was established, entitled *Mercator*. Defoe denied being the author—that is, conductor or editor of this paper—and said that he had not power to put what he would into it; which may have been literally true. Every number, however, bears traces of his hand or guidance; *Mercator* is identical in opinions, style, and spirit with the *Review*, differing only in the greater openness of its attacks upon the opposition of the Whigs to the Treaty of Commerce. Party spirit was so violent that summer, after the publication of the terms of the Treaty of Utrecht, that Defoe was probably glad to shelter himself under the responsibility of another name; he had flaunted the cloak of impartial advice till it had become a thing of shreds and patches.

To prove that the balance of trade, in spite of a prevailing impression to the contrary, not only might be, but had been, on the side of England, was the chief purpose of *Mercator*. The Whig *Flying Post* chaffed *Mercator* for trying to reconcile impossibilities, but *Mercator* held stoutly on with an elaborate apparatus of comparative tables of exports and imports, and ingenious schemes for the development of various branches of the trade with France. Defoe was too fond of carrying the war into the enemy's country, to attack prohibitions or the received doctrine as to the balance of trade in principle; he fought the enemy spiritedly on their own ground. "Take a medium of three years for above forty years past, and calculate the exports and imports to and from France, and it shall appear the balance of trade was always on the English side, to the loss and disadvantage of the French." It followed, upon the received commercial doctrines, that the French King was making a great concession in consenting to take off high duties upon English goods. This was precisely what Defoe was labouring to prove. "The French King in taking off the said high duties ruins all his own manufactures." The common belief was that the terms of peace would ruin English manufacturing industry; full in the teeth of this, Defoe, as was his daring custom, flung the parodox of the extreme opposite. On this occasion he acted purely as a party writer. That he was never a free-trader, at least in principle, will appear from the following extract from his *Plan of the English Commerce*, published in 1728 :—

"Seeing trade then is the fund of wealth and power, we cannot wonder that we see the wisest Princes and States anxious and concerned for the increase of the commerce and trade of their subjects, and of the growth of the country; anxious to propagate the sale of such goods as are the manufacture of their own subjects, and that employs their own people; especially of such as keep the money of their dominions at home ; and on the contrary, for prohibiting the importation from abroad of such things as are the product of other countries, and of the labour of other people, or which carry money back in return, and not merchandise in exchange.

'· Nor can we wonder that we see such Princes and States endeavouring to set up such manufactures in their own countries, which they see successfully and profitably carried on by their neighbours, and to endeavour to procure the materials proper for setting up those manufactures by all just and possible methods from other countries..

"Hence we cannot blame the French or Germans for endeavouring to get over the British wool into their hands, by the help of which they may bring their people to imitate our manufactures, which are so esteemed in the world, as well as so gainful at home.

"Nor can we blame any foreign nation for prohibiting the use and wearing of our manufactures, if they can either make them at home, or make any which they can shift with in their stead.

"The reason is plain. 'Tis the interest of every nation to encourage their own trade, to encourage those manufactures that will employ their own subjects, consume their own growth of provisions, as well as materials of commerce, and such as will keep their money or species at home.

'Tis from this just principle that the French prohibit the English woollen manufacture, and the English again prohibit, or impose a tax equal to a prohibition, on the French silks, paper, linen, and several other of their manufactures. 'Tis from the same just reason in trade that we prohibit the wearing of East India wrought silks, printed calicoes, &c.; that we prohibit the importation of French brandy, Brazil sugars, and Spanish tobacco ; and so of several other things."

CHAPTER VII.

DIFFICULTIES IN RE-CHANGING SIDES.

DEFOE'S unwearied zeal in the service of Harley had excited the bitterest resentment among his old allies, the Whigs. He often complained of it, more in sorrow than in anger. He had no right to look for any other treatment; it was a just punishment upon him for seeking the good of his country without respect of parties. An author that wrote from principle had a very hard task in those dangerous times. If he ventured on the dangerous precipice of telling unbiassed truth, he must expect martyrdom from both sides. This resignation of the simple single-minded patriot to the pains and penalties of honesty, naturally added to the rage of the party with whose factious proceedings he would have nothing to do; and yet it has always been thought an extraordinary instance of party spite that the Whigs should have instituted a prosecution against him, on the alleged ground that a certain remarkable series of Tracts were written in favour of the Pretender. Towards the end of 1712 Defoe had issued *A Seasonable Warning and Caution against the Insinuations of Papists and Jacobites in favour of the Pretender.* No charge of

Jacobitism could be made against a pamphlet containing such a sentence as this :—

"Think, then, dear Britons! what a King this Pretender must be! a papist by inclination; a tyrant by education; a Frenchman by honour and obligation;—and how long will your liberties last you in this condition? And when your liberties are gone, how long will your religion remain? When your hands are tied; when armies bind you; when power oppresses you; when a tyrant disarms you; when a Popish French tyrant reigns over you; by what means or methods can you pretend to maintain your Protestant religion?"

A second pamphlet, *Hannibal at the Gates*, strongly urging party union and the banishment of factious spirit, was equally unmistakable in tone. The titles of the following three of the series were more startling :— *Reasons against the Succession of the House of Hanover— And what if the Pretender should come? or Some considerations of the advantages and real consequences of the Pretender's possessing the Crown of Great Britain—An Answer to a Question that nobody thinks of, viz. But what if the Queen should die?* The contents, however, were plainly ironical. The main reason against the Succession of the Prince of Hanover was that it might be wise for the nation to take a short turn of a French, Popish, hereditary-right *régime* in the first place as an emetic. Emetics were good for the health of individuals, and there could be no better preparative for a healthy constitutional government than another experience of arbitrary power. Defoe had used the same ironical argument for putting Tories in office in 1708. The advantages of the Pretender's possessing the Crown were that we should be saved from all further danger of

a war with France, and should no longer hold the
exposed position of a Protestant State among the
great Catholic Powers of Europe. The point of the last
pamphlet of the series was less distinct; it suggested
the possibility of the English people losing their pro-
perties, their estates, inheritance, lands, goods, lives,
and liberties, unless they were clear in their own minds
what course to take in the event of the Queen's death.
But none of the three Tracts contain anything that
could possibly be interpreted as a serious argument in
favour of the Pretender. They were all calculated to
support the Succession of the Elector of Hanover. Why,
then, should the Whigs have prosecuted the author? It
was a strange thing, as Defoe did not fail to complain,
that they should try to punish a man for writing in their
own interest.

The truth, however, is that although Defoe afterwards
tried to convince the Whig leaders that he had written
these pamphlets in their interest, they were written in the
interest of Harley. They were calculated to recommend
that Minister to Prince George, in the event of his
accession to the English throne. We see this at once
when we examine their contents by the light of the
personal intrigues of the time. Harley was playing a
double game. It was doubtful who the Queen's successor would be, and he aimed at making himself safe
in either of the two possible contingencies. Very soon
after his accession to power in 1710, he made vague overtures for the restoration of the Stuarts under guarantees
for civil and religious liberty. When pressed to take
definite steps in pursuance of this plan, he deprecated
haste, and put off and put off, till the Pretender's
adherents lost patience. All the time he was making

protestations of fidelity to the Court of Hanover. The increasing vagueness of his promises to the Jacobites seems to show that, as time went on, he became convinced that the Hanoverian was the winning cause. No man could better advise him as to the feeling of the English people than Defoe, who was constantly perambulating the country on secret services, in all probability for the direct purpose of sounding the general opinion. It was towards the end of 1712, by which time Harley's shilly-shallying had effectually disgusted the Jacobites, that the first of Defoe's series of Anti-Jacobite tracts appeared. It professed to be written by An Englishman at the Court of Hanover, which affords some ground, though it must be confessed slight, for supposing that Defoe had visited Hanover, presumably as the bearer of some of Harley's assurances of loyalty. The *Seasonable Warning and Caution* was circulated, Defoe himself tells us, in thousands among the poor people by several of his friends. Here was a fact to which Harley could appeal as a circumstantial proof of his zeal in the Hanoverian cause. Whether Defoe's Anti-Jacobite tracts really served his benefactor in this way, can only be matter of conjecture. However that may be, they were upon the surface written in Harley's interest. The warning and caution was expressly directed against the insinuations that the Ministry were in favour of the Pretender. All who made these insinuations were assumed by the writer to be Papists, Jacobites, and enemies of Britain. As these insinuations were the chief war-cry of the Whigs, and we now know that they were not without foundation, it is easy to understand why Defoe's pamphlets, though Anti-Jacobite, were resented by the party in whose interest he had formerly written. He excused

himself afterwards by saying that he was not aware of the
Jacobite leanings of the Ministry; that none of them ever
said one word in favour of the Pretender to him; that
he saw no reason to believe that they did favour the
Pretender. As for himself, he said, they certainly never
employed him in any Jacobite intrigue. He defied his
enemies to "prove that he ever kept company or had
any society, friendship, or conversation with any Jacobite. So averse had he been to the interest and the
people, that he had studiously avoided their company on
all occasions." Within a few months of his making
these protestations, Defoe was editing a Jacobite newspaper under secret instructions from a Whig Government. But this is anticipating.

That an influential Whig should have set on foot a
prosecution of Defoe as the author of "treasonable libels
against the House of Hanover," although the charge had
no foundation in the language of the incriminated
pamphlets, is intelligible enough. The Whig party
writers were delighted with the prosecution, one of them
triumphing over Defoe as being caught at last, and
put "in Lob's pound," and speaking of him as "the
vilest of all the writers that have prostituted their pens
either to encourage faction, oblige a party, or serve their
own mercenary ends." But that the Court of Queen's
Bench, before whom Defoe was brought—with some
difficulty, it would appear, for he had fortified his house
at Newington like Robinson Crusoe's castle—should
have unanimously declared his pamphlets to be treasonable, and that one of them, on his pleading that they were
ironical, should have told him it was a kind of irony for
which he might come to be hanged, drawn, and quar-
tered, is not so easy to understand, unless we suppose

that in these tempestuous times, judges like other men
were powerfully swayed by party feeling. It is possible,
however, that they deemed the mere titles of the
pamphlets offences in themselves, disturbing cries raised
while the people were not yet clear of the forest of
anarchy, and still subject to dangerous panics—offences
of the same nature as if a man should shout fire in
sport in a crowded theatre. Possibly, also, the severity
of the Court was increased by Defoe's indiscretion in
commenting upon the case in the *Review*, while it was
still *sub judice*. At any rate he escaped punishment.
The Attorney-General was ordered to prosecute him, but
before the trial came off Defoe obtained a pardon under
the royal seal.

The Whigs were thus baulked of revenge upon their
renegade. Their loyal writers attributed Defoe's pardon to the secret Jacobitism of the Ministry—quite
wrongly—as we have just seen he was acting for Harley
as a Hanoverian and not as a Jacobite. Curiously
enough, when Defoe next came before the Queen's
Bench, the instigator of the prosecution was a Tory,
and the Government was Whig, and he again escaped
from the clutches of the law by the favour of the
Government. Till Mr. William Lee's remarkable discovery fourteen years ago of certain letters in Defoe's
handwriting in the State Paper Office, it was generally
believed that on the death of Queen Anne, the fall of
the Tory Administration, and the complete discomfiture
of Harley's trimming policy, the veteran pamphleteer
and journalist, now fifty-three years of age, withdrew
from political warfare, and spent the evening of his
life in the composition of those works of fiction which
have made his name immortal. His biographers had

misjudged his character and underrated his energy. When Harley fell from power, Defoe sought service under the Whigs. He had some difficulty in regaining their favour, and when he did obtain employment from them, it was of a kind little to his honour.

In his *Appeal to Honour and Justice*, published early in 1715, in which he defended himself against the charges copiously and virulently urged of being a party-writer, a hireling, and a turncoat, and explained everything that was doubtful in his conduct by alleging the obligations of gratitude to his first benefactor Harley, Defoe declared that since the Queen's death he had taken refuge in absolute silence. He found, he said, that if he offered to say a word in favour of the Hanoverian settlement, it was called fawning and turning round again, and therefore he resolved to meddle neither one way nor the other. He complained sorrowfully that in spite of this resolution, and though he had not written one book since the Queen's death, a great many things were called by his name. In that case, he had no resource but to practise a Christian spirit and pray for the forgiveness of his enemies. This was Defoe's own account, and it was accepted as the whole truth, till Mr. Lee's careful research and good fortune gave a different colour to his personal history from the time of Harley's displacement.[1]

During the dissensions in the last days of the Queen which broke up the Tory Ministry, *Mercator* was dropped.

---

[1] In making mention of Mr. Lee's valuable researches and discoveries, I ought to add that his manner of connecting the facts for which I am indebted to him, and the construction he puts upon them, is entirely different from mine. For the view here implied of Defoe's character and motives, Mr. Lee is in no way responsible.

Defoe seems immediately to have entered into communication with the printer of the Whig *Flying Post*, one William Hurt. The owner of the *Post* was abroad at the time, but his managers, whether actuated by personal spite or reasonable suspicion, learning that Hurt was in communication with one whom they looked upon as their enemy, decided at once to change their printer. There being no copyright in newspaper titles in those days, Hurt retaliated by engaging Defoe to write another paper under the same title, advertising that, from the arrangements he had made, readers would find the new *Flying Post* better than the old. It was in his labours on this sham *Flying Post*, as the original indignantly called it in an appeal to Hurt's sense of honour and justice against the piracy, that Defoe came into collision with the law. His new organ was warmly loyal. On the 14th of August it contained a highly-coloured panegyric of George I., which alone would refute Defoe's assertion that he knew nothing of the arts of the courtier. His Majesty was described as a combination of more graces, virtues, and capacities than the world had ever seen united in one individual, a man "born for council and fitted to command the world." Another number of the *Flying Post*, a few days afterwards, contained an attack on one of the few Tories among the Lords of the Regency, nominated for the management of affairs till the King's arrival. During Bolingbroke's brief term of ascendency, he had despatched the Earl of Anglesey on a mission to Ireland. The Earl had hardly landed at Dublin when news followed him of the Queen's death, and he returned to act as one of the Lords Regent. In the *Flying Post* Defoe asserted that the object of his journey to Ireland was "to new model the Forces there, and particularly to break no less than seventy of the honest officers of the army, and to fill up their places with the tools and creatures of Con. Phipps, and such a rabble of cut-throats as were fit for the work that they had for them to do." That there was some truth in the allegation is likely enough; Sir Constantine Phipps was, at least, shortly afterwards dismissed from his offices.   But Lord Anglesey at once took action against it as a scandalous libel.   Defoe was brought before the Lords Justices, and committed for trial.

He was liberated, however, on bail, and in spite of what he says about his resolution not to meddle on either side, made an energetic use of his liberty.   He wrote *The Secret History of One Year*—the year after William's accession—vindicating the King's clemency towards the abettors of the arbitrary government of James, and explaining that he was compelled to employ many of them by the rapacious scrambling of his own adherents for places and pensions.   The indirect bearing of this tract is obvious.   In October three pamphlets came from Defoe's fertile pen; an *Advice to the People of England* to lay aside feuds and faction, and live together under the new King like good Christians; and two parts, in quick succession, of a *Secret History of the White Staff*. This last work was an account of the circumstances under which the Treasurer's White Staff was taken from the Earl of Oxford, and put his conduct in a favourable light, exonerating him from the suspicion of Jacobitism, and affirming—not quite accurately, as other accounts of the transaction seem to imply—that it was by Harley's advice that the Staff was committed to the Earl of Shrewsbury.   One would be glad to accept this as proof of Defoe's attachment to the cause of his disgraced benefactor; yet Harley, as he lay in the Tower awaiting his trial on an impeachment of high treason, issued a disclaimer concerning the *Secret History* and another pamphlet, entitled, *An Account of the Conduct of Robert, Earl of Oxford.* These pamphlets, he said, were not written with his knowledge or by his direction or encouragement; "on the contrary, he had reason to believe from several passages therein contained that it was the intention of the author, or authors, to do him a prejudice." This disclaimer may have been dictated by a wish not to appear wanting in respect to his judges; at any rate Defoe's *Secret History* bears no trace on the surface of a design to prejudice him by its recital of facts. *An Appeal to Honour and Justice* was Defoe's next production. While writing it, he was seized with a violent apoplectic fit, and it was issued with a Conclusion by the Publisher, mentioning this circumstance, explaining that the pamphlet was consequently incomplete, and adding: "If he recovers, he may be able to finish what he began; if not, it is the opinion of most that know him that the treatment which he here complains of, and some others that he would have spoken of, have been the apparent cause of his disaster." There is no sign of incompleteness in the *Appeal;* and the Conclusion by the Publisher, while the author lay "in a weak and languishing condition, neither able to go on nor likely to recover, at least in any short time," gives a most artistic finishing stroke to it. Defoe never interfered with the perfection of it after his recovery, which took place very shortly. The *Appeal* was issued in the first week of January; before the end of the month the indomitable writer was ready with a Third Part of the

Secret History, and a reply to Atterbury's *Advice to the Freeholders of England* in view of the approaching elections. A series of tracts written in the character of a Quaker quickly followed, one rebuking a Dissenting preacher for inciting the new Government to vindictive severities, another rebuking Sacheverell for hypocrisy and perjury in taking the oath of abjuration, a third rebuking the Duke of Ormond for encouraging Jacobite and High Church mobs. In March Defoe published his *Family Instructor*, a book of 450 pages; in July, his *History, by a Scots Gentleman in the Swedish Service, of the Wars of Charles XII.*

Formidable as the list of these works seems, it does not represent more than Defoe's average rate of production for thirty years of his life. With grave anxieties added to the strain of such incessant toil, it is no wonder that nature should have raised its protest in an apoplectic fit. Even nature must have owned herself vanquished, when she saw this very protest pressed into the service of the irresistible and triumphant worker. All the time he was at large upon bail, awaiting his trial. The trial took place in July, 1715, and he was found guilty. But sentence was deferred till next term. October came round, but Defoe did not appear to receive his sentence. He had made his peace with the Government, upon " capitulations " of which chance has preserved the record in his own handwriting. He represented privately to Lord Chief Justice Parker that he had always been devoted to the Whig interest, and that any seeming departure from it had been due to errors of judgment, not to want of attachment. Whether the Whig leaders believed this representation we do not know, but they agreed to pardon "all former mistakes'

I 2

if he would now enter faithfully into their service.
Though the Hanoverian succession had been cordially
welcomed by the steady masses of the nation, the Mar
Rebellion in Scotland and the sympathy shown with this
movement in the south, warned them that their enemies
were not to be despised.   There was a large turbulent
element in the population, upon which agitators might
work with fatal effect.   The Jacobites had still a hold
upon the Press, and the past years had been fruitful of
examples of the danger of trying to crush sedition with
the arm of the law.   Prosecution had been proved to be
the surest road to popularity.   It occurred therefore
that Defoe might be useful if he still passed as an
opponent of the Government, insinuated himself as such
into the confidence of Jacobites, obtained control of
their publications, and nipped mischief in the bud.   It
was a dangerous and delicate service, exposing the
emissary to dire revenge if he were detected, and to
suspicion and misconstruction from his employers in his
efforts to escape detection.   But Defoe, delighting in
his superior wits, and happy in the midst of dangerous
intrigues, boldly undertook the task.

CHAPTER VIII.

FOR the discovery of this "strange and surprising" chapter in Defoe's life, which clears up much that might otherwise have been disputable in his character, the world is indebted solely to Mr. William Lee. Accident put Mr. Lee on the right scent, from which previous biographers had been diverted by too literal and implicit a faith in the arch-deceiver's statements, and too comprehensive an application of his complaint that his name was made the hackney title of the times, upon which all sorts of low scribblers fathered their vile productions. Defoe's secret services on Tory papers exposed him, as we have seen, to misconstruction. Nobody knew this better than himself, and nobody could have guarded against it with more sleepless care. In the fourth year of King George's reign a change took place in the Ministry. Lord Townshend was succeeded in the Home Secretary's office by Lord Stanhope. Thereupon Defoe judged it expedient to write to a private secretary, Mr. de la Faye, explaining at length his position. This letter along with five others, also designed to prevent misconstruction by his employers, lay in the State Paper Office till the year 1864, when

the whole packet fell into the hands of Mr. Lee. The
following succinct fragment of autobiography is dated
April 26, 1718.

"Though I doubt not but you have acquainted my Lord
Stanhope with what humble sense of his lordship's goodness I
received the account you were pleased to give me, that my little
services are accepted, and that his lordship is satisfied to go
upon the foot of former capitulations, &c.; yet I confess, Sir,
I have been anxious upon many accounts, with respect as
well to the service itself as my own safety, lest my lord
may think himself ill-served by me, even when I have best
performed my duty.

"I thought it therefore not only a debt to myself, but a
duty to his lordship, that I should give his lordship a short
account, as clear as I can, how far my former instructions
empowered me to act, and in a word what this little piece of
service is, for which I am so much a subject of his lordship's
present favour and bounty.

"It was in the Ministry of my Lord Townshend, when my
Lord Chief Justice Parker, to whom I stand obliged for the
favour, was pleased so far to state my case, that notwithstanding the misrepresentations under which I had suffered, and
notwithstanding some mistakes which I was the first to
acknowledge, I was so happy as to be believed in the professions I made of a sincere attachment to the interest of
the present Government, and, speaking with all possible
humility, I hope I have not dishonoured my Lord Parker's
recommendation.

"In considering, after this, which way I might be rendered
most useful to the Government, it was proposed by my Lord
Townshend that I should still appear as if I were, as before,
under the displeasure of the Government, and separated from
the Whigs ; and that I might be more serviceable in a kind
of disguise than if I appeared openly ; and upon this foot a
weekly paper, which I was at first directed to write, in opposition to a scandalous paper called the *Shift Shifted*, was laid
aside, and the first thing I engaged in was a monthly book

called *Mercurius Politicus,* of which presently. In the interval of this, Dyer, the *News-Letter* writer, having been dead, and Dormer, his successor, being unable by his troubles to carry on that work, I had an offer of a share in the property, as well as in the management of that work.

"I immediately acquainted my Lord Townshend of it, who, by Mr. Buckley, let me know it would be a very acceptable piece of service ; for that letter was really very prejudicial to the public, and the most difficult to come at in a judicial way in case of offence given. My lord was pleased to add, by Mr. Buckley, that he would consider my service in that case, as he afterwards did.

"Upon this I engaged in it ; and that so far, that though the property was not wholly my own, yet the conduct and government of the style and news was so entirely in me, that I ventured to assure his lordship the sting of that mischievous paper should be entirely taken out, though it was granted that the style should continue Tory as it was, that the party might be amused and not set up another, which would have destroyed the design, and this part I therefore take entirely on myself still.

"This went on for a year, before my Lord Townshend went out of the office ; and his lordship, in consideration of this service, made me the appointment which Mr. Buckley knows of, with promise of a further allowance as service presented.

"My Lord Sunderland, to whose goodness I had many years ago been obliged, when I was in a secret commission sent to Scotland, was pleased to approve and continue this service, and the appointment annexed ; and with his lordship's approbation, I introduced myself, in the disguise of a translator of the foreign news, to be so far concerned in this weekly paper of *Mist's* as to be able to keep it within the circle of a secret management, also prevent the mischievous part of it ; and yet neither Mist, or any of those concerned with him, have the least guess or suspicion by whose direction I do it.

"But here it becomes necessary to acquaint my lord (as I hinted to you, Sir), that this paper, called the *Journal,* is not

in myself in property, as the other, only in management ;
with this express difference, that if anything happens to be
put in without my knowledge, which may give offence, or if
anything slips my observation which may be ill-taken, his
lordship shall be sure always to know whether he has a
servant to reprove or a stranger to correct.

"Upon the whole, however, this is the consequence, that
by this management, the weekly *Journal*, and *Dormer's
Letter*, as also the *Mercurius Politicus*, which is in the same
nature of management as the *Journal*, will be always kept
(mistakes excepted) to pass as Tory papers, and yet be dis-
abled and enervated, so as to do no mischief or give any
offence to the Government."

Others of the tell-tale letters show us in detail how
Defoe acquitted himself of his engagements to the
Government—bowing, as he said, in the house of
Rimmon. In one he speaks of a traitorous pamphlet
which he has stopped at the press, and begs the Secretary to assure his superiors that he has the original in
safe keeping, and that no eye but his own has seen it.
In another he apologizes for an obnoxious paragraph
which had crept into *Mist's Journal*, avowing that
" Mr. Mist did it, after I had looked over what he had
gotten together," that he [Defoe] had no concern in it,
directly or indirectly, and that he thought himself
obliged to notice this, to make good what he said in his
last, viz. that if any mistake happened, Lord Stanhope
should always know whether he had a servant to reprove or a stranger to punish. In another he expresses
his alarm at hearing of a private suit against Morphew,
the printer of the *Mercurius Politicus*, for a passage
in that paper, and explains, first, that the obnoxious
passage appeared two years before, and was consequently
covered by a capitulation giving him indemnity for

all former mistakes; secondly, that the thing itself
was not his, neither could any one pretend to charge it
on him, and consequently it could not be adduced as
proof of any failure in his duty.   In another letter he
gives an account of a new treaty with Mist.   "I need
not trouble you," he says, "with the particulars, but in
a word he professes himself convinced that he has been
wrong, that the Government has treated him with lenity
and forbearance, and he solemnly engages to me to give
no more offence.   The liberties Mr. Buckley mentioned,
viz. to seem on the same side as before, to rally the
Flying Post, the Whig writers, and even the word
'Whig,' &c., and to admit foolish and trifling things
in favour of the Tories.   This, as I represented it to
him, he agrees is liberty enough, and resolves his paper
shall, for the future, amuse the Tories, but not affront
the Government."   If Mist should break through this
understanding, Defoe hopes it will be understood that
it is not his fault; he can only say that the printer's
resolutions of amendment seem to be sincere.

"In pursuance also of this reformation, he brought me this
morning the enclosed letter, which, indeed, I was glad to see,
because, though it seems couched in terms which might have
been made public, yet has a secret gall in it, and a manifest
tendency to reproach the Government with partiality and
injustice, and (as it acknowledges expressly) was written to
serve a present turn.   As this is an earnest of his just intention, I hope he will go on to your satisfaction.

"Give me leave, Sir, to mention here a circumstance
which concerns myself, and which, indeed, is a little hardship
upon me, viz. that I seem to merit less, when I intercept a
piece of barefaced treason at the Press, than when I stop
such a letter as the enclosed; because one seems to be of a
kind which no man would dare to meddle with.   But I would

persuade myself, Sir, that stopping such notorious things is not
without its good effect, particularly because, as it is true that
some people are generally found who do venture to print anything that offers, so stopping them here is some discouragement and disappointment to them, and they often die in our
hands.

" I speak this, Sir, as well on occasion of what you were
pleased to say upon that letter which I sent you formerly
about *Killing no Murder*, as upon another with verses in it,
which Mr. Mist gave me yesterday ; which, upon my word,
is so villainous and scandalous that I scarce dare to send it
without your order, and an assurance that my doing so shall
be taken well, for I confess it has a peculiar insolence in it
against His Majesty's person which (as blasphemous words
against God) are scarce fit to be repeated."

In the last of the series (of date June 13, 1718),
Defoe is able to assure his employers that " he believes
the time is come when the journal, instead of affronting
and offending the Government, may many ways be made
serviceable to the Government ; and he has Mr. M. so
absolutely resigned to proper measures for it, that he
is persuaded he may answer for it."

Following up the clue afforded by these letters, Mr.
Lee has traced the history of *Mist's Journal* under
Defoe's surveillance.   Mist did not prove so absolutely
resigned to proper measures as his supervisor had
begun to hope.   On the contrary, he had frequent fits of
refractory obstinacy, and gave a good deal of trouble
both to Defoe and to the Government.   Between them,
however, they had the poor man completely in their
power.   When he yielded to the importunity of his
Jacobite correspondents, or kicked against the taunts
of the Whig organs about his wings being clipped,—
they, no more than he, knew how—his secret controllers

had two ways of bringing him to reason. Sometimes the
Government prosecuted him, wisely choosing occasions
for their displeasure on which they were likely to have
popular feeling on their side. At other times Defoe
threatened to withdraw and have nothing more to do
with the *Journal*. Once or twice he carried this threat
into execution. His absence soon told on the circulation, and Mist entreated him to return, making promises
of good behaviour for the future. Further, Defoe
commended himself to the gratitude of his unconscious
dupe by sympathizing with him in his troubles, undertaking the conduct of the paper while he lay in prison,
and editing two volumes of a selection of *Miscellany
Letters* from its columns. At last, however, after eight
years of this partnership, during which Mist had no
suspicion of Defoe's connexion with the Government,
the secret somehow seems to have leaked out. Such
at least is Mr. Lee's highly probable explanation of a
murderous attack made by Mist upon his partner.

Defoe, of course, stoutly denied Mist's accusations, and
published a touching account of the circumstances,
describing his assailant as a lamentable instance of
ingratitude. Here was a man whom he had saved from
the gallows, and befriended at his own risk in the
utmost distress, turning round upon him, "basely using,
insulting, and provoking him, and at last drawing his
sword upon his benefactor." Defoe disarmed him, gave
him his life, and sent for a surgeon to dress his wounds.
But even this was not enough. Mist would give him
nothing but abuse of the worst and grossest nature.
It almost shook Defoe's faith in human nature. Was
there ever such ingratitude known before? The most
curious thing is that Mr. Lee, who has brought all

these facts to light, seems to share Defoe's ingenuous
astonishment at this "strange instance of ungrateful
violence," and conjectures that it must have proceeded
from imaginary wrong of a very grievous nature, such
as a suspicion that Defoe had instigated the Government
to prosecute him.   It is perhaps as well that it should
have fallen to so loyal an admirer to exhume Defoe's
secret services and public protestations; the record
might otherwise have been rejected as incredible.

Mr. Lee's researches were not confined to Defoe's
relations with Mist and his journal, and the other publications mentioned in the precious letter to Mr. de la
Faye.   Once assured that Defoe did not withdraw from
newspaper-writing in 1715, he ransacked the journals
of the period for traces of his hand and contemporary
allusions to his labours.   A rich harvest rewarded Mr.
Lee's zeal.   Defoe's individuality is so marked that it
thrusts itself through every disguise.   A careful student
of the *Review*, who had compared it with the literature
of the time, and learnt his peculiar tricks of style and
vivid ranges of interest, could not easily be at fault in
identifying a composition of any length.   Defoe's incomparable clearness of statement would alone betray him;
that was a gift of nature which no art could successfully
imitate.   Contemporaries also were quick at recognising
their Proteus in his many shapes, and their gossip gives
a strong support to internal evidence, resting as it probably did on evidences which were not altogether internal.   Though Mr. Lee may have been rash sometimes
in quoting little scraps of news as Defoe's, he must be
admitted to have established that, prodigious as was the
number and extent of the veteran's separate publications
during the reign of the First George, it was also the

most active period of his career as a journalist. Managing Mist and writing for his journal would have been work enough for an ordinary man, but Defoe founded, conducted, and wrote for a host of other newspapers— the monthly *Mercurius Politicus*, an octavo of sixty-four pages (1716—1720); the weekly *Dormer's Newsletter* (written, not printed, 1716—1718); the *Whitehall Evening Post* (a tri-weekly quarto-sheet, established 1718); the *Daily Post* (a daily single leaf, folio, established 1719); and *Applebee's Journal* (with which his connexion began in 1720 and ended in 1726).

The contributions to these newspapers which Mr. Lee has assigned, with great judgment it seems to me, to Defoe, range over a wide field of topics, from piracy and highway robberies to suicide and the Divinity of Christ. Defoe's own test of a good writer was that he should at once please and serve his readers, and he kept this double object in view in his newspaper writings, as much as in *Robinson Crusoe, Moll Flanders*, and the *Family Instructor*. Great as is the variety of subjects in the selections which Mr. Lee has made upon internal evidence, they are all of them subjects in which Defoe showed a keen interest in his acknowledged works. In providing amusement for his readers he did not soar above his age in point of refinement; and in providing instruction, he did not fall below his age in point of morality and religion. It is a notable circumstance that one of the marks by which contemporaries traced his hand was "the little art he is truly master of, of forging a story and imposing it on the world for truth." Of this he gave a conspicuous instance in *Mist's Journal* in an account of the marvellous blowing up of the island of St. Vincent, which in circumstantial invention and force of description must be ranked among his master-pieces. But Defoe did more than embellish stories of strange events for his newspapers. He was a master of journalistic art in all its branches, and a fertile inventor and organizer of new devices. It is to him, Mr. Lee says, and his researches entitle him to authority, that we owe the prototype of the leading article, a Letter Introductory, as it became the fashion to call it, written on some subject of general interest and placed at the commencement of each number. The writer of this Letter Introductory was known as the "author" of the paper.

Another feature in journalism which Defoe greatly helped to develop, if he did not actually invent, was the Journal of Society. In the *Review* he had provided for the amusement of his readers by the device of a Scandal Club, whose transactions he professed to report. But political excitement was intense throughout the whole of Queen Anne's reign; Defoe could afford but small space for scandal, and his Club was often occupied with fighting his minor political battles. When, however, the Hanoverian succession was secured, and the land had rest from the hot strife of parties, light gossip was more in request. Newspapers became less political, and their circulation extended from the coffee-houses, inns, and ale-houses to a new class of readers. "They have of late," a writer in *Applebee's Journal* says in 1725, "been taken in much by the women, especially the political ladies, to assist at the tea-table." Defoe seems to have taken an active part in making *Mist's Journal* and *Applebee's Journal*, both Tory organs, suitable for this more frivolous section of the public This fell in with his purpose of diminishing the political weight of these journals, and at the same time increased their sale. He converted them from rabid party agencies into registers of domestic news and vehicles of social disquisitions, sometimes grave, sometimes gay in subject, but uniformly bright and spirited in tone.

The raw materials of several of Defoe's elaborate tales, such as *Moll Flanders* and *Colonel Jack*, are to be found in the columns of *Mist's* and *Applebee's*. In connexion with *Applebee's* more particularly, Defoe went some way towards anticipating the work of the modern Special Correspondent. He apparently interviewed distinguished criminals in Newgate, and extracted from them the stories of their lives. Part of what he thus gathered he communicated to *Applebee;* sometimes, when the notoriety of the case justified it, he drew up longer narratives and published them separately as pamphlets. He was an adept in the art of puffing his own productions, whether books or journals. It may be doubted whether any American editor ever mastered this art more thoroughly than Defoe. Nothing, for instance, could surpass the boldness of Defoe's plan for directing public attention to his narrative of the robberies and escapes of Jack Sheppard. He seems to have taken a particular interest in this daring gaol-breaker. Mr. Lee, in fact, finds evidence that he had gained Sheppard's affectionate esteem. He certainly turned his acquaintance to admirable account. He procured a letter for *Applebee's Journal* from Jack, with "kind love," and a copy of verses of his own composition. Both letter and verses probably came from a more practised pen, but, to avert suspicion, the original of the letter was declared to be on view at Applebee's, and "well known to be in the handwriting of John Sheppard." Next Defoe prepared a thrilling narrative of Jack's adventures, which was of course described as written by the prisoner himself, and printed at his particular desire. But this was not all. The artful author further arranged that when Sheppard reached his place of execution, he should send for a friend to the cart as he stood under the gibbet, and deliver a copy of the pamphlet as his last speech and dying confession. A paragraph recording this incident was duly inserted in the newspapers. It is a crowning illustration of the inventive daring with which Defoe practised the tricks of his trade.

One of Defoe's last works in connection with journalism was to write a prospectus for a new weekly periodical, the *Universal Spectator*, which was started by his son-in-law, Henry Baker, in October 1728. There is more than internal and circumstantial evidence that this prospectus was Defoe's composition. When Baker retired from the paper five years afterwards, he drew up a list of the articles which had appeared under his editorship, with the names of the writers attached. This list has been preserved, and from it we learn that the first number, containing a prospectus and an introductory essay on the qualifications of a good writer, was written by Defoe. That experienced journalist naturally tried to give an air of novelty to the enterprise. "If this paper," the first sentence runs, "was not intended to be what no paper at present is, we should never attempt to crowd in among such a throng of public writers as at this time oppress the town." In effect the scheme of the *Universal Spectator* was to revive the higher kind of periodical essays which made the reputation of the earlier *Spectator.* Attempts to follow in the wake of Addison and Steele had for so long ceased to be features in journalism; their manner had been so effectually superseded by less refined purveyors of light literature—Defoe himself going heartily with the stream—that the revival was opportune, and in point of fact proved successful, the *Universal Spectator* continuing to exist for nearly twenty years. It shows how quickly the *Spectator* took its place among the classics, that the writer of the prospectus considered it necessary to deprecate a charge of presumption in seeming to challenge comparison.

" Let no man envy us the celebrated title we have assumed, or charge us with arrogance, as if we bid the world expect great things from us. Must we have no power to please, unless we come up to the full height of those inimitable performances? Is there no wit or humour left because they are gone? Is the spirit of the *Spectators* all lost, and their mantle fallen upon nobody? Have they said all that can be said? Has the world offered no variety, and presented no new scenes, since they retired from us? Or did they leave off, because they were quite exhausted, and had no more to say? "

Defoe did not always speak so respectfully of the authors of the *Spectator*. If he had been asked why they left off, he would probably have given the reason contained in the last sentence, and backed his opinion by contemptuous remarks about the want of fertility in the scholarly brain. He himself could have gone on producing for ever; he was never gravelled for lack of matter, had no nice ideas about manner, and was sometimes sore about the superior respectability of those who had. But here he was on business, addressing people who looked back regretfully from the vulgarity of *Mist's* and *Applebee's* to the refinement of earlier periodicals, and making a bid for their custom. A few more sentences from his advertisement will show how well he understood their prejudices :—

"The main design of this work is, to turn your thoughts a little off from the clamour of contending parties, which has so long surfeited you with their ill-timed politics, and restore your taste to things truly superior and sublime.

"In order to this, we shall endeavour to present you with such subjects as are capable, if well handled, both to divert and to instruct you ; such as shall render conversation pleasant, and help to make mankind agreeable to one another.

"As for our management of them, not to promise too much for ourselves, we shall only say we hope, at least, to make our work acceptable to everybody, because we resolve, if possible to displease nobody.

"We assure the world, by way of negative, that we shall engage in no quarrels, meddle with no parties, deal in no scandal, nor endeavour to make any men merry at the expense of their neighbours. In a word, we shall set nobody together by the ears. And though we have encouraged the ingenious world to correspond with us by letters, we hope they will not take it ill, that we say beforehand, no letters will be taken notice of by us which contain any personal reproaches, intermeddle with family breaches, or tend to scandal or indecency of any kind.

"The current papers are more than sufficient to carry on all the dirty work the town can have for them to do ; and what with party strife, politics, poetic quarrels, and all the other consequences of a wrangling age ; they are in no danger of wanting employment ; and those readers who delight in such things, may divert themselves there. But our views, as is said above, lie another way."

Good writing is what Defoe promises the readers of the *Universal Spectator*, and this leads him to

consider what particular qualifications go to the composition, or in a word, "what is required to denominate
a man a *good writer*." His definition is worth quoting
as a statement of his principles of composition.

"One says this is a polite author ; another says, that is an
excellent *good-writer* ; and generally we find some oblique
strokes pointed sideways at themselves ; intimating that
whether we think fit to allow it or not, they take themselves
to be very *good writers*. And, indeed, I must excuse them
their vanity ; for if a poor author had not some good opinion
of himself, especially when under the discouragement of
having nobody else to be of his mind, he would never write
at all ; nay, he could not ; it would take off all the little dull
edge that his pen might have on it before, and he would not
be able to say one word to the purpose.

"Now whatever may be the lot of this paper, be that as
common fame shall direct, yet without entering into the
enquiry who writes better, or who writes worse, I shall lay
down one specific, by which you that read shall impartially
determine who are, or are not, to be called *good writers*. In a
word, the character of a good writer, wherever he is to be
found, is this, viz., that he writes so as to please and serve
at the same time.

"If he writes to *please*, and not to *serve*, he is a flatterer and
a hypocrite ; if to *serve* and not to *please*, he turns cynic and
satirist. The first deals in smooth falsehood, the last in
rough scandal ; the last may do some good, though little ; the
first does no good, and may do mischief, not a little ; the last
provokes your rage, the first provokes your pride ; and in a
word either of them is hurtful rather than useful. But the
writer that strives to be useful, writes to *serve* you, and at
the same time, by an imperceptible art, draws you on to be
pleased also. He represents truth with plainness, virtue with
praise ; he even reprehends with a softness that carries the
force of a satire without the salt of it ; and he insensibly
screws himself into your good opinion, that as his writings
merit your regard, so they fail not to obtain it.

K 2

"This is part of the character by which I define a good
writer; I say 'tis but part of it, for it is not a half sheet that
would contain the full description; a large volume would
hardly suffice it. His fame requires, indeed, a very good
writer to give it due praise; and for that reason (and a good
reason too) I go no farther with it."

CHAPTER IX.

THOSE of my readers who have thought of Defoe only as a writer of stories which young and old still love to read, must not be surprised that so few pages of this little book should be left for an account of his work in that field. No doubt Defoe's chief claim to the world's interest is that he is the author of *Robinson Crusoe*. But there is little to be said about this or any other of Defoe's tales in themselves. Their art is simple, unique, incommunicable, and they are too well known to need description. On the other hand, there is much that is worth knowing and not generally known about the relation of these works to his life, and the place that they occupy in the sum total of his literary activity. Hundreds of thousands since Defoe's death, and millions in ages to come, would never have heard his name but for *Robinson Crusoe*. To his contemporaries the publication of that work was but a small incident in a career which for twenty years had claimed and held their interest. People in these days are apt to imagine, because Defoe wrote the most fascinating of books for children, that he was himself simple, child-like, frank, open, and unsuspecting. He has been so described by

more than one historian of literature. It was not so
that he appeared to his contemporaries, and it is not so
that he can appear to us when we know his life, unless
we recognise that he took a child's delight in beating
with their own weapons the most astute intriguers in
the most intriguing period of English history.

Defoe was essentially a journalist. He wrote for
the day, and for the greatest interest of the greatest
number of the day. He always had some ship sailing
with the passing breeze, and laden with a useful cargo
for the coast upon which the wind chanced to be blowing. If the Tichborne trial had happened in his time,
we should certainly have had from him an exact history
of the boyhood and surprising adventures of Thomas
Castro, commonly known as Sir Roger, which would
have come down to us as a true record, taken, perhaps,
by the chaplain of Portland prison from the convict's
own lips. It would have had such an air of authenticity,
and would have been corroborated by such an array of
trustworthy witnesses, that nobody in later times could
have doubted its truth. Defoe always wrote what a
large number of people were in a mood to read. All
his writings, with so few exceptions that they may
reasonably be supposed to fall within the category, were
pièces de circonstance. Whenever any distinguished
person died or otherwise engaged public attention, no
matter how distinguished, whether as a politician, a
criminal, or a divine, Defoe lost no time in bringing
out a biography. It was in such emergencies that he
produced his memoirs of Charles XII., Peter the Great,
Count Patkul, the Duke of Shrewsbury, Baron de Goertz,
the Rev. Daniel Williams, Captain Avery the King of
the Pirates, Dominique Cartouche, Rob Roy, Jonathan

Wild, Jack Sheppard, Duncan Campbell. When the day had been fixed for the Earl of Oxford's trial for high treason, Defoe issued the fictitious *Minutes of the Secret Negotiations of Mons. Mesnager* at the English Court during his ministry. We owe the *Journal of the Plague in 1665* to a visitation which fell upon France in 1721, and caused much apprehension in England. The germ which in his fertile mind grew into *Robinson Crusoe* fell from the real adventures of Alexander Selkirk, whose solitary residence of four years on the island of Juan Fernandez was a nine days' wonder in the reign of Queen Anne. Defoe was too busy with his politics at the moment to turn it to account; it was recalled to him later on, in the year 1719, when the exploits of famous pirates had given a vivid interest to the chances of adventurers in far-away islands on the American and African coasts. The *Life, Adventures, and Piracies of the famous Captain Singleton*, who was set on shore in Madagascar, traversed the continent of Africa from east to west past the sources of the Nile, and went roving again in the company of the famous Captain Avery, was produced to satisfy the same demand. Such biographies as those of *Moll Flanders* and the *Lady Roxana* were of a kind, as he himself illustrated by an amusing anecdote, that interested all times and all professions and degrees; but we have seen to what accident he owed their suggestion and probably part of their materials. He had tested the market for such wares in his Journals of Society.

In following Defoe's career, we are constantly reminded that he was a man of business, and practised the profession of letters with a shrewd eye to the main chance. He scoffed at the idea of practising it with any other

object, though he had aspirations after immortal fame
as much as any of his more decorous contemporaries.
Like Thomas Fuller, he frankly avowed that he wrote
" for some honest profit to himself." Did any man, he
asked, do anything without some regard to his own
advantage ? Whenever he hit upon a profitable vein,
he worked it to exhaustion, putting the ore into various
shapes to attract different purchasers. *Robinson Crusoe*
made a sensation; he immediately followed up the
original story with a Second Part, and the Second Part
with a volume of *Serious Reflections*. He had discovered
the keenness of the public appetite for stories of the
supernatural, in 1706, by means of his *True Relation of
the Apparition of one Mrs. Veal*.[1] When, in 1720, he
undertook to write the life of the popular fortune-teller,
Duncan Campbell—a puff which illustrates almost better
than anything else Defoe's extraordinary ingenuity in
putting a respectable face upon the most disreputable
materials—he had another proof of the avidity with
which people run to hear marvels. He followed up
this clue with *A System of Magic, or a History of the
Black Art; The Secrets of the Invisible World disclosed,
or a Universal History of Apparitions;* and a humorous
History of the Devil, in which last work he subjected
Paradise Lost, to which Addison had drawn attention

---

[1] Mr. Lee has disposed conclusively of the myth that this tale
was written to promote the sale of a dull book by one Drelincourt
on the *Fear of Death*, which Mrs. Veal's ghost earnestly recommended her friend to read. It was first published separately as a
pamphlet without any reference to Drelincourt. It was not printed
with Drelincourt's *Fear of Death* till the fourth edition of that
work, which was already popular. Further, the sale of Drelincourt
does not appear to have been increased by the addition of Defoe's
pamphlet to the book; and of Mrs. Veal's recommendation to the
pamphlet.

by his papers in the *Spectator*, to very sharp criticism. In his books and pamphlets on the Behaviour of Servants, and his works of more formal instruction, the *Family Instructor*, the *Plan of English Commerce*, the *Complete English Tradesman*, the *Complete English Gentleman* (his last work, left unfinished and unpublished), he wrote with a similar regard to what was for the moment in demand.

Defoe's novel-writing thus grew naturally out of his general literary trade, and had not a little in common with the rest of his abundant stock. All his productions in this line, his masterpiece, *Robinson Crusoe*, as well as what Charles Lamb calls his "secondary novels," *Captain Singleton*, *Colonel Jack*, *Moll Flanders*, and *Roxana*, were manufactured from material for which he had ascertained that there was a market; the only novelty lay in the mode of preparation. From writing biographies with real names attached to them, it was but a short step to writing biographies with fictitious names. Defoe is sometimes spoken of as the inventor of the realistic novel ; realistic biography would, perhaps, be a more strictly accurate description. Looking at the character of his professed records of fact, it seems strange that he should ever have thought of writing the lives of imaginary heroes, and should not have remained content with "forging stories and imposing them on the world for truth" about famous and notorious persons in real life. The purveyors of news in those days could use without fear of detection a licence which would not be tolerated now. They could not, indeed, satisfy the public appetite for news without taking liberties with the truth. They had not special correspondents in all parts of the world, to fill their pages with reports from the spot of things seen and heard. The public had acquired

the habit of looking to the press, to periodical papers
and casual books and pamphlets, for information about
passing events and prominent men before sufficient
means had been organized for procuring information
which should approximate to correctness.   In such circumstances, the temptation to invent and embellish was
irresistible.   "Why," a paragraph-maker of the time is
made to say, "If we will write nothing but truth, we
must bring you no news ; we are bound to bring you such
as we can find."   Yet it was not lies but truth that the
public wanted as much as they do now.   Hence arose
the necessity of fortifying reports with circumstantial
evidence of their authenticity.   Nobody rebuked un-
principled news-writers more strongly than Defoe, and
no news-writer was half as copious in his guarantees for
the accuracy of his information.   When a report reached
England that the island of St. Vincent had been blown
into the air, Defoe wrote a description of the calamity,
the most astonishing thing that had happened in the
world "since the Creation, or at least since the destruc-
tion of the earth by water in the general Deluge," and
prefaced his description by saying :—

"Our accounts of this come from so many several hands and
several places that it would be impossible to bring the letters
all separately into this journal ; and when we had done so, or attempted to do so, would leave the story confused, and the world
not perfectly informed.   We have therefore thought it better
to give the substance of this amazing accident in one collection;
making together as full and as distinct an account of the whole
as we believe it possible to come at by any intelligence whatsoever, and at the close of this account we shall give some probable guesses at the natural cause of so terrible an operation."

Defoe carried the same system of vouching for the
truth of his narratives by referring them to likely

sources, into pamphlets and books which really served
the purpose of newspapers, being written for the gratification of passing interests.   The History of the Wars
of Charles XII., which Mr. Lee ascribes to him, was
written " by a Scots gentleman, in the Swedish service."
The short narrative of the life and death of Count
Patkul was- " written by the Lutheran Minister who
assisted him in his last hours, and faithfully translated
out of a High Dutch manuscript." M. Mesnager's minutes
of his negotiations were " written by himself," and " done
out of French." Defoe knew that the public would
read such narratives more eagerly if they believed them
to be true, and ascribed them to authors whose position
entitled them to confidence.   There can be little doubt
that he drew upon his imagination for more than the
title-pages.   But why when he had so many eminent
and notorious persons to serve as his subjects, with all
the advantage of bearing names about which the public
were already curious, did he turn to the adventures of
new and fictitious heroes and heroines ?   One can
only suppose that he was attracted by the greater free
dom of movement in pure invention ; he made the
venture with *Robinson Crusoe*, it was successful, and he
repeated it.   But after the success of *Robinson Crusoe*,
he by no means abandoned his old fields.   It was after
this that he produced autobiographies and other *primâ
facie* authentic lives of notorious thieves and pirates.
With all his records of heroes, real or fictitious, he
practised the same devices for ensuring credibility.   In
all alike he took for granted that the first question
people would ask about a story was whether it was true.
the novel, it must be remembered, was then in its
infancy, and Defoe, as we shall presently see, imagined,

probably not without good reason, that his readers would disapprove of story-telling for the mere pleasure of the thing, as an immorality.

In writing for the entertainment of his own time, Defoe took the surest way of writing for the entertainment of all time. Yet if he had never chanced to write *Robinson Crusoe*, he would now have a very obscure place in English literature. His "natural infirmity of homely plain writing," as he humorously described it, might have drawn students to his works, but they ran considerable risk of lying in utter oblivion. He was at war with the whole guild of respectable writers who have become classics; they despised him as an illiterate fellow, a vulgar huckster, and never alluded to him except in terms of contempt. He was not slow to retort their civilities; but the retorts might very easily have sunk beneath the waters, while the assaults were preserved by their mutual support. The vast mass of Defoe's writings received no kindly aid from distinguished contemporaries to float them down the stream; everything was done that bitter dislike and supercilious indifference could do to submerge them. *Robinson Crusoe* was their sole life-buoy.

It would be a mistake to suppose that the vitality of *Robinson Crusoe* is a happy accident, and that others of Defoe's tales have as much claim in point of merit to permanence. *Robinson Crusoe* has lived longest, because it lives most, because it was detached as it were from its own time and organized for separate existence. It is the only one of Defoe's tales that shows what he could do as an artist. We might have seen from the others that he had the genius of a great artist; here we have the possibility realized, the convincing proof of accomplished work.

Moll Flanders is in some respects superior as a novel. Moll is a much more complicated character than the simple, open-minded, manly mariner of York; a strangely mixed compound of craft and impulse, selfishness and generosity—in short, a thoroughly bad woman, made bad by circumstances. In tracing the vigilant resolution with which she plays upon human weakness, the spasms of compunction which shoot across her wily designs, the selfish afterthoughts which paralyse her generous impulses, her fits of dare-devil courage and uncontrollable panic, and the steady current of good-humoured satisfaction with herself which makes her chuckle equally over mishaps and successes, Defoe has gone much more deeply into the springs of action, and sketched a much richer page in the natural history of his species than in *Robinson Crusoe*. True, it is a more repulsive page, but that is not the only reason why it has fallen into comparative oblivion, and exists now only as a parasite upon the more popular work. It is not equally well constructed for the struggle of existence among books. No book can live for ever which is not firmly organized round some central principle of life, and that principle in itself imperishable. It must have a heart and members; the members must be soundly compacted and the heart superior to decay. Compared with *Robinson Crusoe*, *Moll Flanders* is only a string of diverting incidents, the lowest type of book organism, very brilliant while it is fresh and new, but not qualified to survive competitors for the world's interest. There is no unique creative purpose in it to bind the whole together; it might be cut into pieces, each capable of wriggling amusingly by itself. The gradual corruption of the heroine's virtue, which is the encompassing scheme of the tale, is too thin as well as too common an artistic envelope; the incidents burst through it at so many points that it becomes a shapeless mass. But in *Robinson Crusoe* we have real growth from a vigorous germ. The central idea round which the tale is organized, the position of a man cast ashore on a desert island, abandoned to his own resources, suddenly shot beyond help or counsel from his fellow-creatures, is one that must live as long as the uncertainty of human life.

The germ of *Robinson Crusoe*, the actual experience of Alexander Selkirk, went floating about for several years, and more than one artist dallied with it, till it finally settled and took root in the mind of the one man of his generation most capable of giving it a home and working out its artistic possibilities. Defoe was the only man of letters in his time who might have been thrown on a desert island without finding himself at a loss what to do. The art required for developing the position in imagination was not of a complicated kind, and yet it is one of the rarest of gifts. Something more was wanted than simply conceiving what a man in such a situation would probably feel and probably do. Above all, it was necessary that his perplexities should be unexpected, and his expedients for meeting them unexpected; yet both perplexities and expedients so real and life-like that, when we were told them, we should wonder we had not thought of them before. One gift was indispensable for this, however many might be accessory, the genius of circumstantial invention—not a very exalted order of genius, perhaps, but quite as rare as any other intellectual prodigy.[1]

[1] Mr. Leslie Stephen seems to me to underrate the rarity of this peculiar gift in his brilliant essay on Defoe's Novels in *Hours in a Library*.

Defoe was fifty-eight years old when he wrote *Robinson Crusoe*. If the invention of plausible circumstances is the great secret in the art of that tale, it would have been a marvellous thing if this had been the first instance of its exercise, and it had broken out suddenly in a man of so advanced an age. When we find an artist of supreme excellence in any craft, we generally find that he has been practising it all his life. To say that he has a genius for it, means that he has practised it, and concentrated his main force upon it, and that he has been driven irresistibly to do so by sheer bent of nature. It was so with Defoe and his power of circumstantial invention, his unrivalled genius for "lying like truth." For years upon years of his life it had been his chief occupation. From the time of his first connexion with Harley, at least, he had addressed his countrymen through the press, and had perambulated the length and breadth of the land in assumed characters and on factitious pretexts. His first essay in that way in 1704, when he left prison in the service of the Government, appealing to the general compassion because he was under government displeasure, was skilful enough to suggest great native genius if not extensive previous practice. There are passages of circumstantial invention in the *Review*, as ingenious as anything in *Robinson Crusoe ;* and the mere fact that at the end of ten years of secret service under successive Governments, and in spite of a widespread opinion of his untrustworthiness, he was able to pass himself off for ten years more as a Tory with Tories and with the Whig Government as a loyal servant, is a proof of sustained ingenuity of invention greater than many volumes of fiction.

Looking at Defoe's private life, it is not difficult to

understand the peculiar fascination which such a pro-
blem as he solved in *Robinson Crusoe* must have had for
him.   It was not merely that he had passed a life of
uncertainty, often on the verge of precipices, and often
saved from ruin by a buoyant energy which seems almost
miraculous ; not merely that, as he said of himself in
one of his diplomatic appeals for commiseration,

> "No man hath tasted differing fortunes more,
>   For thirteen times have I been rich and poor."

But when he wrote *Robinson Crusoe*, it was one of the
actual chances of his life, and by no means a remote
one, that he might be cast all alone on an uninhabited
island.   We see from his letters to De la Faye how
fearful he was of having "mistakes" laid to his charge
by the Government in the course of his secret services.
His former changes of party had exposed him, as he
well knew, to suspicion.   A false step, a misunderstood
paragraph, might have had ruinous consequences for him.
If the Government had prosecuted him for writing anything offensive to them, refusing to believe that it was
put in to amuse the Tories, transportation might very
easily have been the penalty.   He had made so many
enemies in the Press that he might have been transported
without a voice being raised in his favour, and the mob
would not have interfered to save a Government spy
from the Plantations.   Shipwreck among the islands of
the West Indies was a possibility that stood not far from
his own door, as he looked forward into the unknown,
and prepared his mind as men in dangerous situations
do for the worst.   When he drew up for Moll Flanders
and her husband a list of the things necessary for starting life in a new country, or when he described Colonel

Jack's management of his plantation in Virginia, the subject was one of more than general curiosity to him; and when he exercised his imagination upon the fate of Robinson Crusoe, he was contemplating a fate which a few movements of the wheel of Fortune might make his own.

But whatever it was that made the germ idea of *Robinson Crusoe* take root in Defoe's mind, he worked it out as an artist. Artists of a more emotional type might have drawn much more elaborate and affecting word-pictures of the mariner's feelings in various trying situations, gone much deeper into his changing moods, and shaken our souls with pity and terror over the solitary castaway's alarms and fits of despair. Defoe's aims lay another way. His Crusoe is not a man given to the luxury of grieving. If he had begun to pity himself, he would have been undone. Perhaps Defoe's imaginative force was not of a kind that could have done justice to the agonies of a shipwrecked sentimentalist; he has left no proof that it was; but if he had represented Crusoe bemoaning his misfortunes, brooding over his fears, or sighing with Ossianic sorrow over his lost companions and friends, he would have spoiled the consistency of the character. The lonely man had his moments of panic and his days of dejection, but they did not dwell in his memory. Defoe no doubt followed his own natural bent, but he also showed true art in confining Crusoe's recollections as closely as he does to his efforts to extricate himself from difficulties that would have overwhelmed a man of softer temperament. The subject had fascinated him, and he found enough in it to engross his powers without travelling beyond its limits for diverting episodes, as he does more

L

or less in all the rest of his tales. The diverting
episodes in *Robinson Crusoe* all help the verisimilitude
of the story.

When, however, the ingenious inventor had completed the story artistically, carried us through all the
outcast's anxieties and efforts, and shown him triumphant
over all difficulties, prosperous, and again in communication with the outer world, the spirit of the literary
trader would not let the finished work alone. The
story, as a work of art, ends with Crusoe's departure
from the island, or at any rate with his return to
England. Its unity is then complete. But Robinson
Crusoe at once became a popular hero, and Defoe was
too keen a man of business to miss the chance of further
profit from so lucrative a vein. He did not mind the
sneers of hostile critics. They made merry over the
trifling inconsistencies in the tale. How, for example.
they asked, could Crusoe have stuffed his pockets with
biscuits when he had taken off all his clothes before
swimming to the wreck? How could he have been at
such a loss for clothes after those he had put off were
washed away by the rising tide, when he had the ship's
stores to choose from? How could he have seen the
goat's eyes in the cave when it was pitch dark? How
could the Spaniards give Friday's father an agreement
in writing, when they had neither paper nor ink? How
did Friday come to know so intimately the habits of
bears, the bear not being a denizen of the West Indian
islands? On the ground of these and such-like trifles,
one critic declared that the book seems calculated for
the mob, and will not bear the eye of a rational reader,
and that "all but the very canaille are satisfied of the
worthlessness of the performance." Defoe, we may

suppose, was not much moved by these strictures, as edition after edition of the work was demanded. He corrected one or two little inaccuracies, and at once set about writing a Second Part, and a volume of *Serious Reflections* which had occurred to Crusoe amidst his adventures. These were purely commercial excrescences upon the original work. They were popular enough at the time, but those who are tempted now to accompany Crusoe in his second visit to his island and his enter-prising travels in the East, agree that the Second Part is of inferior interest to the first, and very few now read the *Serious Reflections.*

The *Serious Reflections,* however, are well worth reading in connexion with the author's personal history. In the preface we are told that *Robinson Crusoe* is an allegory, and in one of the chapters we are told why it is an allegory. The explanation is given in a homily against the vice of talking falsely. By talking falsely the moralist explains that he does not mean telling lies, that is, falsehoods concocted with an evil object; these he puts aside as sins altogether beyond the pale of discussion. But there is a minor vice of falsehood which he considers it his duty to reprove, namely, telling stories, as too many people do, merely to amuse. "This supplying a story by invention," he says, "is certainly a most scandalous crime, and yet very little regarded in that part. It is a sort of lying that makes a great hole in the heart, in which by degrees a habit of lying enters in. Such a man comes quickly up to a total disregarding the truth of what he says, looking upon it as a trifle, a thing of no import, whether any story he tells be true or not." How empty a satisfaction is this " purchased at so great an expense as that of conscience, and of a

dishonour done to truth !" And the crime is so entirely
objectless. A man who tells a lie, properly so called,
has some hope of reward by it. But to lie for sport is
to play at shuttlecock with your soul, and load your
conscience for the mere sake of being a fool. "With
what temper should I speak of those people? What
words can express the meanness and baseness of the
mind that can do this?" In making this protest against
frivolous story-telling, the humour of which must have
been greatly enjoyed by his journalistic colleagues,
Defoe anticipated that his readers would ask why, if he
so disapproved of the supplying a story by invention,
he had written *Robinson Crusoe*. His answer was that
Robinson Crusoe was an allegory, and that the telling
or writing a parable or an allusive allegorical history is
quite a different case. "I, Robinson Crusoe, do affirm
that the story, though allegorical, is also historical, and
that it is the beautiful representation of a life of
unexampled misfortunes, and of a variety not to be met
with in this world." This life was his own. He explains
at some length the particulars of the allegory :—

"Thus the fright and fancies which succeeded the story of
the print of a man's foot, and surprise of the old goat, and
the thing rolling on my bed, and my jumping up in a fright,
are all histories and real stories ; as are likewise the dream of
being taken by messengers, being arrested by officers, the
manner of being driven on shore by the surge of the sea, the
ship on fire, the description of starving, the story of my man
Friday, and many more most natural passages observed here,
and on which any religious reflections are made, are all historical and true in fact. It is most real that I had a parrot,
and taught it to call me by my name, such a servant a savage
and afterwards a Christian, and that his name was called
Friday, and that he was ravished from me by force, and died

in the hands that took him, which I represent by being killed; this is all literally true, and should I enter into discoveries many alive can testify them. His other conduct and assistance to me also have just references in all their parts to the helps I had from that faithful savage in my real solitudes and disasters.

"The story of the bear in the tree, and the fight with the wolves in the snow, is likewise matter of real history; and in a word, the adventures of Robinson Crusoe are a whole scheme of a life of twenty-eight years spent in the most wandering, desolate, and afflicting circumstances that ever man went through, and in which I have lived so long in a life of wonders, in continued storms, fought with the worst kind of savages and man-eaters, by unaccountable surprising incidents; fed by miracles greater than that of the ravens, suffered all manner of violences and oppressions, injurious reproaches, contempt of men, attacks of devils, corrections from Heaven, and oppositions on earth ; and had innumerable ups and downs in matters of fortune, been in slavery worse than Turkish, escaped by an exquisite management, as that in the story of Xury and the boat of Sallee, been taken up at sea in distress, raised again and depressed again, and that oftener perhaps in one man's life than ever was known before ; shipwrecked often, though more by land than by sea ; in a word, there's not a circumstance in the imaginary story but has its just allusion to a real story, and chimes part for part, and step for step, with the inimitable life of Robinson Crusoe."

But if Defoe had such a regard for the strict and literal truth, why did he not tell his history in his own person? Why convey the facts allusively in an allegory? To this question also he had an answer. He wrote for the instruction of mankind, for the purpose of recommending " invincible patience under the worst of misery ; indefatigable application and undaunted resolution under the greatest and most discouraging circumstances."

"Had the common way of writing a man's private history been taken, and I had given you the conduct or life of a man you knew, and whose misfortunes and infirmities perhaps you had sometimes unjustly triumphed over, all I could have said would have yielded no diversion, and perhaps scarce have obtained a reading, or at best no attention ; the teacher, like a greater, having no honour in his own country."

For all Defoe's profession that *Robinson Crusoe* is an allegory of his own life, it would be rash to take what he says too literally. The reader who goes to the tale in search of a close allegory, in minute chronological correspondence with the facts of the alleged original, will find, I expect, like myself, that he has gone on a wild-goose chase. There is a certain general correspondence. Defoe's own life is certainly as instructive as Crusoe's in the lesson of invincible patience and undaunted resolution. The shipwreck perhaps corresponds with his first bankruptcy, with which it coincides in point of time, having happened just twenty-eight years before. If Defoe had a real man Friday, who had learnt all his arts till he could practise them as well as himself, the fact might go to explain his enormous productiveness as an author. But I doubt whether the allegory can be pushed into such details. Defoe's fancy was quick enough to give an allegorical meaning to any tale. He might have found in Moll Flanders, with her five marriages and ultimate prostitution, corresponding to his own five political marriages and the dubious conduct of his later years, a closer allegory in some respects than in the life of the shipwrecked sailor. The idea of calling *Robinson Crusoe* an allegory was in all probability an afterthought, perhaps suggested by a derisive parody which had appeared, entitled *The life and strange*

surprising adventures of Daniel de Foe, of London, Hosier,
who lived all alone in the uninhabited island of Great
Britain, and so forth.

If we study any writing of Defoe's in connexion with
the circumstances of its production, we find that it is
manysided in its purposes, as full of side aims as a nave
is full of spokes.   These supplementary moral chapters
to *Robinson Crusoe*, admirable as the reflections are in
themselves, and naturally as they are made to arise out
of the incidents of the hero's life, contain more than
meets the eye till we connect them with the author's
position.   Calling the tale an allegory served him in
two ways.   In the first place, it added to the interest of
the tale itself by presenting it in the light of a riddle,
which was left but half-revealed, though he declared
after such explanation as he gave that "the riddle was
now expounded, and the intelligent reader might see
clearly the end and design of the whole work."   In
the second place, the allegory was such an image of his
life as he wished for good reasons to impress on the
public mind.   He had all along, as we have seen, while
in the secret service of successive governments, vehemently protested his independence, and called Heaven
and Earth to witness that he was a poor struggling,
unfortunate, calumniated man.   It was more than ever
necessary now when people believed him to be under the
insuperable displeasure of the Whigs, and he was really
rendering them such dangerous service in connexion
with the Tory journals, that he should convince the
world of his misfortunes and his honesty.   The *Serious
Reflections* consist mainly of meditations on Divine
Providence in times of trouble, and discourses on the
supreme importance of honest dealing.   They are put

into the mouth of Robinson Crusoe, but the reader is warned that they occurred to the author himself in the midst of real incidents in his own life. Knowing what public repute said of him, he does not profess never to have strayed from the paths of virtue, but he implies that he is sincerely repentant, and is now a reformed character. " Wild wicked Robinson Crusoe does not pretend to honesty himself." He acknowledges his early errors. Not to do so would be a mistaken piece of false bravery. "All shame is cowardice. The bravest spirit is the best qualified for a penitent. He, then, that will be honest, must dare to confess that he has been a knave."   But the man that has been sick is half a physician, and therefore he is both well fitted to counsel others, and being convinced of the sin and folly of his former errors, is of all men the least likely to repeat them. Want of courage was not a feature in Defoe's diplomacy. He thus boldly described the particular form of dishonesty with which, when he wrote the description, he was practising upon the unconscious Mr. Mist.

"There is an ugly word called cunning, which is very per-nicious to it [honesty], and which particularly injures it by hiding it from our discovery and making it hard to find. This is so like honesty that many a man has been deceived with it, and have taken one for t'other in the markets : nay, I have heard of some who have planted this *wild honesty*, as we may call it, in their own ground, have made use of it in their friendship and dealings, and thought it had been the true plant. But they always lost credit by it, and that was not the worst neither, for they had the loss who dealt with them, and who chaffered for a counterfeit commodity ; and we find many deceived so still, which is the occasion there is such an outcry about false friends, and about sharping and tricking in men's ordinary dealings with the world."

A master-mind in the art of working a man, as
Bacon calls it, is surely apparent here. Who could
have suspected the moralist of concealing the sins he
was inclined to, by exposing and lamenting those very
sins ? There are other passages in the *Serious Reflections*
which seem to have been particularly intended for
Mist's edification. In reflecting what a fine thing
honesty is, Crusoe expresses an opinion that it is much
more common than is generally supposed, and gratefully
recalls how often he has met with it in his own
experience. He asks the reader to note how faithfully
he was served by the English sailor's widow, the
Portuguese captain, the boy Xury, and his man Friday.
From these allegoric-types, Mist might select a model
for his own behaviour. When we consider the tone of
these *Serious Reflections,* so eminently pious, moral, and
unpretending, so obviously the outcome of a wise, simple,
ingenuous nature, we can better understand the fury
with which Mist turned upon Defoe when at last he
discovered his treachery. They are of use also in throwing light upon the prodigious versatility which could dash
off a masterpiece in fiction, and, before the printer's ink
was dry, be already at work making it a subordinate
instrument in a much wider and more wonderful scheme
of activity, his own restless life.

It is curious to find among the *Serious Reflections,* a
passage which may be taken as an apology for the practices into which Defoe, gradually, we may reasonably
believe, allowed himself to fall. The substance of the
apology has been crystallized into an aphorism by the
author of Becky Sharp, but it has been, no doubt, the
consoling philosophy of dishonest persons not altogether
devoid of conscience in all ages.

"Necessity makes an honest man a knave; and if the world was to be the judge, according to the common received notion, there would not be an honest poor man alive.

"A rich man is an honest man, no thanks to him, for he would be a double knave to cheat mankind when he had no need of it. He has no occasion to prey upon his integrity, nor so much as to touch upon the borders of dishonesty. Tell me of a man that is a very honest man; for he pays everybody punctually, runs into nobody's debt, does no man any wrong; very well, what circumstances is he in? Why, he has a good estate, a fine yearly income, and no business to do. The Devil must have full possession of this man, if he should be a knave; for no man commits evil for the sake of it; even the Devil himself has some farther design in sinning, than barely the wicked part of it. No man is so hardened in crimes as to commit them for the mere pleasure of the fact; there is always some vice gratified; ambition, pride, or avarice makes rich men knaves, and necessity the poor."

This is Defoe's excuse for his backslidings put into the mouth of *Robinson Crusoe*. It might be inscribed also on the threshold of each of his fictitious biographies. Colonel Jack, Moll Flanders, Roxana are not criminals from malice; they do not commit crimes for the mere pleasure of the fact. They all believe that but for the force of circumstances they might have been orderly, contented, virtuous members of society. The Colonel, a London Arab, a child of the criminal regiment, began to steal before he knew that it was not the approved way of making a livelihood. Moll and Roxana were overreached by acts against which they were too weak to cope. Even after they were tempted into taking the wrong turning, they did not pursue the downward road without compunction. Many good people might say of them, "There, but for the grace of God, goes myself." But it was not from the point of view of a Baxter or a Bunyan that Defoe regarded them, though he credited them with many edifying reflections. He was careful to say that he would never have written the stories of their lives, if he had not thought that they would be useful as awful examples of the effects of bad education and the indulgence of restlessness and vanity; but he enters into their ingenious shifts and successes with a joyous sympathy that would have been impossible if their reckless adventurous living by their wits had not had a strong charm for him. We often find peeping out in Defoe's writings that roguish cynicism which we should expect in a man whose own life was so far from being straightforward. He was too much dependent upon the public acceptance of honest professions to be eager in depreciating the value of the article, but when he found other people protesting disinterested motives, he could not always resist reminding them that they were no more disinterested than the Jack-pudding who avowed that he cured diseases from mere love of his kind. Having yielded to circumstances himself, and finding life enjoyable in dubious paths, he had a certain animosity against those who had maintained their integrity and kept to the highroad, and a corresponding pleasure in showing that the motives of the sinner were not after all so very different from the motives of the saint.

The aims in life of Defoe's thieves and pirates are at bottom very little different from the ambition which he undertakes to direct in the *Complete English Tradesman,* and their maxims of conduct have much in common with this ideal. Self-interest is on the look-out, and Self-reliance at the helm.

"A tradesman behind his counter must have no flesh and blood about him, no passions, no resentment; he must never be angry—no, not so much as seem to be so, if a customer tumbles him five hundred pounds worth of goods, and scarce bids money for anything; nay, though they really come to his shop with no intent to buy, as many do, only to see what is to be sold, and though he knows they cannot be better pleased than they are at some other shop where they intend to buy, 'tis all one; the tradesman must take it, he must place it to the account of his calling, that 'tis his business to be ill-used, and resent nothing; and so must answer as obligingly to those who give him an hour or two's trouble, and buy nothing, as he does to those who, in half the time, lay out ten or twenty pounds. The case is plain; and if some do give him trouble, and do not buy, others make amends, and do buy; and as for the trouble, 'tis the business of the shop."

All Defoe's heroes and heroines are animated by this practical spirit, this thoroughgoing subordination of means to ends. When they have an end in view, the plunder of a house, the capture of a ship, the ensnaring of a dupe, they allow neither passion, nor resentment, nor sentiment in any shape or form to stand in their way. Every other consideration is put on one side when the business of the shop has to be attended to. They are all tradesmen who have strayed into unlawful courses. They have nothing about them of the heroism of sin; their crimes are not the result of ungovernable passion, or even of antipathy to conventional restraints; circumstances and not any law-defying bias of disposition have made them criminals. How is it that the novelist contrives to make them so interesting? Is it because we are a nation of shop-keepers, and enjoy following lines of business which are a little out of our ordinary routine? Or is it simply that he makes us enjoy their courage and cleverness without thinking of the purposes with which these qualities are displayed? Defoe takes such delight in tracing their bold expedients, their dexterous intriguing and manœuvring, that he seldom allows us to think of anything but the success or failure of their enterprises. Our attention is concentrated on the game, and we pay no heed for the moment to the players or the stakes. Charles Lamb says of *The Complete English Tradesman* that "such is the bent of the book to narrow and to degrade the heart, that if such maxims were as catching and infectious as those of a licentious cast, which happily is not the case, had I been living at that time, I certainly should have recommended to the grand jury of Middlesex, who presented The Fable of the Bees, to have presented this book of Defoe's in preference, as of a far more vile and debasing tendency." Yet if Defoe had thrown the substance of this book into the form of a novel, and shown us a tradesman rising by the sedulous practice of its maxims from errand-boy to gigantic capitalist, it would have been hardly less interesting than his lives of successful thieves and tolerably successful harlots, and its interest would have been very much of the same kind, the interest of dexterous adaptation of means to ends.

CHAPTER X.

" THE best step," Defoe says after describing the character of a deceitful talker, "such a man can take is to lie
on, and this shows the singularity of the crime; it is
a strange expression, but I shall make it out; their
way is, I say, to lie on till their character is completely
known, and then they can lie no longer, for he whom
nobody deceives can deceive nobody, and the essence of
lying is removed; for the description of a lie is that it
is spoken to deceive, or the design is to deceive. Now
he that nobody believes can never lie any more, because
nobody can be deceived by him."

Something like this seems to have happened to Defoe
himself. He touched the summit of his worldly prosperity about the time of the publication of *Robinson
Crusoe* (1719). He was probably richer then than he had
been when he enjoyed the confidence of King William,
and was busy with projects of manufacture and trade. He
was no longer solitary in journalism. Like his hero he
had several plantations, and companions to help him in
working them. He was connected with four journals,
and from this source alone his income must have been
considerable. Besides this he was producing separate

works at the rate, on an average, of six a year, some of them pamphlets, some of them considerable volumes, all of them calculated to the wants of the time, and several of them extremely popular, running through three or four editions in as many months. Then he had his salary from the government, which he delicately hints at in one of his extant letters as being overdue. Further, the advertisement of a lost pocket-book in 1726, containing a list of Notes and Bills in which Defoe's name twice appears, seems to show that he still found time for commercial transactions outside literature.[1] Altogether Defoe was exceedingly prosperous, dropped all pretence of poverty, built a large house at Stoke Newington, with stables and pleasure-grounds, and kept a coach.

We get a pleasant glimpse of Defoe's life at this period from the notes of Henry Baker, the naturalist, who married one of his daughters and received his assistance, as we have seen, in starting *The Universal Spectator*. Baker, originally a bookseller, in 1724 set up a school for the deaf and dumb at Newington. There, according to the notes which he left of his courtship, he made the acquaintance of "Mr. Defoe, a gentleman well known by his writings, who had newly built there a very handsome house, as a retirement from London, and amused his time either in the cultivation of a large and pleasant garden, or in the pursuit of his studies, which he found means of making very profitable." Defoe "was now at least sixty years of age, afflicted with the gout and stone, but retained all his mental faculties entire." The diarist goes on to say that he "met usually at the tea-table his three lovely daughters, who were admired for their beauty, their education, and their prudent

[1] *Lee's Life*, vol. i. pp. 406–7.

conduct; and if sometimes Mr. Defoe's disorders made
company inconvenient, Mr. Baker was entertained by
them either singly or together, and that commonly in
the garden when the weather was favourable." Mr.
Baker fixed his choice on Sophia, the youngest daughter,
and, being a prudent lover, began negotiations about the
marriage portion, Defoe's part in which is also characteristic. "He knew nothing of Mr. Defoe's circumstances, only imagined, from his very genteel way of
living, that he must be able to give his daughter a
decent portion; he did not suppose a large one. On
speaking to Mr. Defoe, he sanctioned his proposals, and
said he hoped he should be able to give her a certain
sum specified; but when urged to the point some time
afterwards, his answer was that formal articles he thought
unnecessary; that he could confide in the honour of Mr.
Baker; that when they talked before, he did not know
the true state of his own affairs; that he found he could
not part with any money at present; but at his death,
his daughter's portion would be more than he had
promised; and he offered his own bond as security."
The prudent Mr. Baker would not take his bond, and
the marriage was not arranged till two years afterwards,
when Defoe gave a bond for £500 payable at his death,
engaging his house at Newington as security.

Very little more is known about Defoe's family,
except that his eldest daughter married a person of the
name of Langley, and that he speculated successfully in
South Sea Stock in the name of his second daughter,
and afterwards settled upon her an estate at Colchester
worth £1020. His second son, named Benjamin, became
a journalist, was the editor of the *London Journal*, and
got into temporary trouble for writing a scandalous

and seditious libel in that newspaper in 1721. A writer in *Applebee's Journal*, whom Mr. Lee identifies with Defoe himself, commenting upon this circumstance, denied the rumour of its being the well-known Daniel Defoe that was committed for the offence. The same writer declared that it was known "that the young Defoe was but a stalking-horse and a tool, to bear the lash and the pillory in their stead, for his wages ; that he was the author of the most scandalous part, but was only made sham proprietor of the whole, to screen the true proprietors from justice."

This son does not appear in a favourable light in the troubles which soon after fell upon Defoe, when Mist discovered his connexion with the Government. Foiled in his assault upon him, Mist seems to have taken revenge by spreading the fact abroad, and all Defoe's indignant denials and outcries against Mist's ingratitude do not seem to have cleared him from suspicion. Thenceforth the printers and editors of journals held aloof from him. Such is Mr. Lee's fair interpretation of the fact that his connexion with *Applebee's Journal* terminated abruptly in March, 1726, and that he is found soon after, in the preface to a pamphlet on *Street Robberies*, complaining that none of the journals will accept his communications. "Assure yourself, gentle reader," he says,[1] "I had not published my project in this pamphlet, could I have got it inserted in any of the journals without feeing the journalists or publishers. I cannot but have the vanity to think they might as well have inserted what I send them, *gratis*, as many things I have since seen in their papers. But I have not only had the mortification to find what I sent rejected, but

[1] Lee's *Life*, vol. i. p. 418.

M

to lose my originals, not having taken copies of what I wrote." In this preface Defoe makes touching allusion to his age and infirmities. He begs his readers to " excuse the vanity of an over-officious old man, if, like Cato, he inquires whether or no before he goes hence and is no more, he can yet do anything for the service of his country." " The old man cannot trouble you long ; take, then, in good part his best intentions, and impute his defects to age and weakness."

This preface was written in 1728 ; what happened to Defoe in the following year is much more difficult to understand, and is greatly complicated by a long letter of his own which has been preserved. Something had occurred, or was imagined by him to have occurred, which compelled him to fly from his home and go into hiding. He was at work on a book to be entitled *The Complete English Gentleman.* Part of it was already in type when he broke off abruptly in September, 1729, and fled. In August, 1730, he sent from a hiding-place, cautiously described as being about two miles from Greenwich, a letter to his son in-law, Baker, which is our only clue to what had taken place. It is so incoherent as to suggest that the old man's prolonged toils and anxieties had at last shaken his reason, though not his indomitable self-reliance. Baker apparently had written complaining that he was debarred from seeing him. " Depend upon my sincerity for this," Defoe answers, " that I am far from debarring you. On the contrary, it would be a greater comfort to me than any I now enjoy that I could have your agreeable visits with safety, and could see both you and my dear Sophia, could it be without giving her the grief of seeing her father *in tenebris,* and under the load of insupportable sorrows." He gives a touching description of the griefs which are preying upon his mind.

"It is not the blow I received from a wicked, perjured, and contemptible enemy that has broken in upon my spirit; which, as she well knows, has carried me on through greater disasters than these. But it has been the injustice, unkindness, and, I must say inhuman, dealing of my own son, which has both ruined my family, and in a word has broken my heart. . . . I depended upon him, I trusted him, I gave up my two dear unprovided children into his hands; but he has no compassion, but suffers them and their poor dying mother to beg their bread at his door, and to crave, as it were an alms, what he is bound under hand and seal, besides the most sacred promises, to supply them with, himself at the same time living in a profusion of plenty. It is too much for me. Excuse my infirmity, I can say no more ; my heart is too full. I only ask one thing of you as a dying request. Stand by them when I am gone, and let them not be wronged while he is able to do them right. Stand by them as a brother ; and if you have anything within you owing to my memory, who have bestowed on you the best gift I have to give, let them not be injured and trampled on by false pretences and unnatural reflections. I hope they will want no help but that of comfort and council; but that they will indeed want, being too easy to be managed by words and promises."

The postscript to the letter shows that Baker had written to him about selling the house, which, it may be remembered, was the security for Mrs. Baker's portion, and had inquired about a policy of assurance. "I wrote you a letter some months ago, in answer to one from you, about selling the house; but you never signified to me whether you received it. I have not the policy of assurance; I suppose my wife, or Hannah, may have it." Baker's ignoring the previous letter about the house seems to signify that it was unsatisfactory. He apparently wished for a personal interview with Defoe. In the beginning of the present letter Defoe had said that, though far from debarring a visit from his son-in-law, circumstances, much to his sorrow, made it impossible that he could receive a visit from anybody. After the charge against his son, which we have quoted, he goes on to explain that it is impossible for him to go to see Mr. Baker. His family apparently had been ignorant of his movements for some time. " I am at a distance from London in Kent; nor have I a lodging in London, nor have I been at that place in the Old Bailey since I wrote you I was removed from it. At present I am weak, having had some fits of a fever that have left me low." He suggests, indeed, a plan by which he might see his son-in-law and daughter. He could not bear to make them a single flying visit. " Just to come and look at you and retire immediately, 'tis a burden too heavy. The parting will be a price beyond the enjoyment." But if they could find a retired lodging for him at Enfield, " where he might not be known, and might have the comfort of seeing them both now and then, upon such a circumstance he could gladly give the days to solitude to have the comfort of half an hour now and then with them both for two or three weeks." Nevertheless, as if he considered this plan out of the question, he ends with a touching expression of grief that, being near his journey's end, he may never see them again. It is impossible to avoid the conclusion that he did not wish to see his son-in-law, and that Baker wished to see him about money matters, and suspected him of evading an interview.

Was this evasion the cunning of incipient madness?
Was his concealing his hiding-place from his son-in-law
an insane development of that self-reliant caution, which
for so many years of his life he had been compelled to
make a habit, in the face of the most serious risks?
Why did he give such an exaggerated colour to the
infamous conduct of his son? It is easy to make out
from the passage I have quoted, what his son's guilt
really consisted in. Defoe had assigned certain property
to the son to be held in trust for his wife and daughters.
The son had not secured them in the enjoyment of this
provision, but maintained them, and gave them words
and promises, with which they were content, that he
would continue to maintain them. It was this that
Defoe called making them "beg their bread at his door,
and crave as if it were an alms" the provision to which
they were legally entitled. Why did Defoe vent his
grief at this conduct in such strong language to his
son-in-law, at the same time enjoining him to make a
prudent use of it? Baker had written to his father-in
law making inquiry about the securities for his wife's
portion; Defoe answers with profuse expressions of
affection, a touching picture of his old age and feeble-
ness, and the imminent ruin of his family through the
possible treachery of the son to whom he has entrusted
their means of support, and an adjuration to his son-in-
law to stand by them with comfort and counsel when
he is gone. The inquiry about the securities he dismisses
in a postscript. He will not sell the house, and he does
not know who has the policy of assurance.

One thing and one thing only shines clearly out of
the obscurity in which Defoe's closing years are wrapt
—his earnest desire to make provision for those members

of his family who could not provide for themselves.
The pursuit from which he was in hiding, was in all probability the pursuit of creditors.   We have seen that
his income must have been large from the year 1718 or
thereabouts, till his utter loss of credit in journalism
about the year 1726 ; but he may have had old debts.
It is difficult to explain otherwise why he should have
been at such pains, when he became prosperous, to assign
property to his children.   There is evidence as early as
1720 of his making over property to his daughter
Hannah, and the letter from which I have quoted shows
that he did not hold his Newington estate in his own
name.   In this letter he speaks of a perjured contemptible enemy as the cause of his misfortunes.   Mr.
Lee conjectures that this was Mist, that Mist had succeeded in embroiling him with the Government by convincing them of treachery in his secret services, and that
this was the hue and cry from which he fled.   But it is
hardly conceivable that the Government could have
listened to charges brought by a man whom they had
driven from the country for his seditious practices.   It
is much more likely that Mist and his supporters had
sufficient interest to instigate the revival of old pecuniary
claims against Defoe.

It would have been open to suppose that the fears
which made the old man a homeless wanderer and fugitive for the last two years of his life, were wholly imaginary, but for the circumstances of his death.   He died
of a lethargy on the 26th of April, 1731, at a lodging in Ropemaker's Alley, Moorfields.   In September,
1733, as the books in Doctors' Commons show, letters of
administration on his goods and chattels were granted
to Mary Brooks, widow, a creditrix, after summoning in

official form the next of kin to appear. Now, if Defoe
had been driven from his home by imaginary fears, and
had baffled with the cunning of insane suspicion the
effects of his family to bring him back, there is no
apparent reason why they should not have claimed his
effects after his death. He could not have died unknown to them, for place and time were recorded in the
newspapers. His letter to his son-in law, expressing
the warmest affection for all his family except his son,
is sufficient to prevent the horrible notion that he might
have been driven forth like Lear by his undutiful children after he had parted his goods among them. If
they had been capable of such unnatural conduct, they
would not have failed to secure his remaining property.
Why, then, were his goods and chattels left to a creditrix? Mr. Lee ingeniously suggests that Mary Brooks
was the keeper of the lodging where he died, and that
she kept his personal property to pay rent and perhaps
funeral expenses. A much simpler explanation, which
covers most of the known facts without casting any un-
warranted reflections upon Defoe's children, is that when
his last illness overtook him he was still keeping out of
the way of his creditors, and that everything belonging
to him in his own name was legally seized. But there
are doubts and difficulties attending any explanation.

Mr. Lee has given satisfactory reasons for believing
that Defoe did not, as some of his biographers have
supposed, die in actual distress. Ropemaker's Alley in
Moorfields was a highly respectable street at the beginning of last century; a lodging there was far from
squalid. The probability is that Defoe subsisted on his
pension from the Government during his last two years
of wandering; and suffering though he was from the

infirmities of age, yet wandering was less of a hardship than it would have been to other men, to one who had been a wanderer for the greater part of his life. At the best it was a painful and dreary ending for so vigorous a life; and unless we pitilessly regard it as a retribution for his moral defects, it is some comfort to think that the old man's infirmities and anxieties were not aggravated by the pressure of hopeless and helpless poverty. Nor do I think that he was as distressed as he represented to his son-in-law by apprehensions of ruin to his family after his death, and suspicions of the honesty of his son's intentions. There is a half insane tone about his letter to Mr. Baker, but a certain method may be discerned in its incoherences. My own reading of it is that it was a clever evasion of his son-in-law's attempts to make sure of his share of the inheritance. We have seen how shifty Defoe was in the original bargaining about his daughter's portion, and we know from his novels what his views were about fortune-hunters, and with what delight he dwelt upon the arts of outwitting them. He probably considered that his youngest daughter was sufficiently provided for by her marriage, and he had set his heart upon making provision for her unmarried sisters. The letter seems to me to be evidence, not so much of fears for their future welfare, as of a resolution to leave them as much as he could. Two little circumstances seem to show that, in spite of his professions of affection, there was a coolness between Defoe and his son-in-law. He wrote only the prospectus and the first article for Baker's paper, the *Universal Spectator*, and when he died, Baker contented himself with a simple intimation of the fact.

If my reading of this letter is right, it might stand as

a type of the most strongly marked characteristic in Defoe's political writings. It was a masterly and utterly unscrupulous piece of diplomacy for the attainment of a just and benevolent end. This may appear strange after what I have said about Defoe's want of honesty, yet one cannot help coming to this conclusion in looking back at his political career before his character underwent its final degradation. He was a great, a truly great liar, perhaps the greatest liar that ever lived. His dishonesty went too deep to be called superficial, yet, if we go deeper still in his rich and strangely mixed nature, we come upon stubborn foundations of conscience. Among contemporary comments on the occasion of his death, there was one which gave perfect expression to his political position. "His knowledge of men, especially those in high life (with whom he was formerly very conversant) had weakened his attachment to any political party; but in the main, he was in the interest of civil and religious liberty, in behalf of which he appeared on several remarkable occasions." The men of the time with whom Defoe was brought into contact, were not good examples to him. The standard of political morality was probably never so low in England as during his lifetime. Places were dependent on the favour of the Sovereign, and the Sovereign's own seat on the throne was insecure; there was no party cohesion to keep politicians consistent, and every man fought for his own hand. Defoe had been behind the scenes, witnessed many curious changes of service, and heard many authentic tales of jealousy, intrigue, and treachery. He had seen Jacobites take office under William, join zealously in the scramble for his favours, and enter into negotiations with the emissaries of James either upon

some fancied slight, or from no other motive than a
desire to be safe, if by any chance the sceptre should
again change hands.   Under Anne he had seen Whig
turn Tory and Tory turn Whig, and had seen statesmen
of the highest rank hold out one hand to Hanover and
another to St. Germains.   The most single-minded man
he had met had been King William himself, and of his
memory he always spoke with the most affectionate
honour.   Shifty as Defoe was, and admirably as he used
his genius for circumstantial invention to cover his
designs, there was no other statesman of his generation
who remained more true to the principles of the Revolution, and to the cause of civil and religious freedom.
No other public man saw more clearly what was for the
good of the country, or pursued it more steadily.   Even
when he was the active servant of Harley, and turned
round upon men who regarded him as their own, the
part which he played was to pave the way for his
patron's accession to office under the House of Hanover.
Defoe did as much as any one man, partly by secret
intrigue, partly through the public press, perhaps as
much as any ten men outside those in the immediate
direction of affairs, to accomplish the two great objects
which William bequeathed to English statesmanship
—the union of England and Scotland, and the succession to the United Kingdom of a Protestant dynasty.
Apart from the field of high politics, his powerful
advocacy was enlisted in favour of almost every prac-
ticable scheme of social improvement that came to
the front in his time.   Defoe cannot be held up as an
exemplar of moral conduct, yet if he is judged by the
measures that he laboured for, and not by the means
that he employed, few Englishmen have lived more

deserving than he of their country's gratitude. He may have been self-seeking and vain-glorious, but in his political life self-seeking and vain-glory were elevated by their alliance with higher and wider aims. Defoe was a wonderful mixture of knave and patriot. Sometimes pure knave seems to be uppermost, sometimes pure patriot, but the mixture is so complex and the energy of the man so restless, that it almost passes human skill to unravel the two elements. The author of *Robinson Crusoe* is entitled to the benefit of every doubt.

THE END.

LONDON: R. CLAY SONS, AND TAYLOR, PRINTERS.

For EU product safety concerns, contact us at Calle de José Abascal, 56–1°,
28003 Madrid, Spain or eugpsr@cambridge.org.

www.ingramcontent.com/pod-product-compliance
Ingram Content Group UK Ltd.
Pitfield, Milton Keynes, MK11 3LW, UK
UKHW012342130625
459647UK00009B/473